CONTENTS

CLASSIC DAILY BREAD

Rye Bread

Servings: 1 Loaf
Ingredients:
- 16 slice bread (2 pounds)
- 1⅔ cups lukewarm water
- ¼ cup + 4 teaspoons Dijon mustard
- 2 tablespoons unsalted butter, melted
- 4 teaspoons sugar
- 1 teaspoon table salt
- 2 cups rye flour
- 2⅔ cups white bread flour
- 1½ teaspoons bread machine yeast
- 12 slice bread (1½ pounds)
- 1¼ cups lukewarm water
- ¼ cup Dijon mustard
- 1½ tablespoons unsalted butter, melted
- 1 tablespoon sugar
- ¾ teaspoon table salt
- 1½ cups rye flour
- 2 cups white bread flour
- 1 teaspoon bread machine yeast

Directions:
1. Choose the size of loaf you would like to make and measure your ingredients.
2. Add the ingredients to the bread pan in the order listed above.
3. Place the pan in the bread machine and close the lid.
4. Turn on the bread maker. Select the White/Basic setting, then the loaf size, and finally the crust color. Start the cycle.
5. When the cycle is finished and the bread is baked, carefully remove the pan from the machine. Use a potholder as the handle will be very hot. Let rest for a few minutes.
6. Remove the bread from the pan and allow to cool on a wire rack for at least 10 minutes before slicing.

Nutrition Info: (Per Serving):Calories 153, fat 2.1 g, carbs 24.8 g, sodium 256 mg, protein 5.2 g

Pumpkin Spice Cake

Servings: 12
Cooking Time: 2 Hours 50 Minutes
Ingredients:
- 1 cup sugar
- 1 cup canned pumpkin
- 1/3 cup vegetable oil
- 1 teaspoon vanilla extract
- 2 eggs
- 1 1/2 cups all-purpose flour
- 2 teaspoons baking powder

- 1/4 teaspoon salt
- 1 teaspoon ground cinnamon
- 1/4 teaspoon ground nutmeg
- 1/8 teaspoon ground cloves
- Shortening, for greasing pan

Directions:
1. Grease bread maker pan and kneading blade generously with shortening.
2. Add all ingredients to the bread maker pan in the order listed above.
3. Select Rapid cycle and press Start.
4. Open the lid three minutes into the cycle and carefully scrape down sides of pan with a rubber spatula; close lid to continue cycle.
5. Cool baked cake for 10 minutes on a wire rack before slicing.

Nutrition Info: Calories: 195, Sodium: 64 mg, Dietary Fiber: 1.3 g, Fat: 7.1 g, Carbs: 31.2 g, Protein: 2.8 g.

Blue Cheese Bread

Servings: 10 - 12
Cooking Time: 3 Hours
Ingredients:
- 3/4 cup warm water
- 1 large egg
- 1 teaspoon salt
- 3 cups bread flour
- 1 cup blue cheese, crumbled
- 2 tablespoons nonfat dry milk
- 2 tablespoons sugar
- 1 teaspoon bread machine yeast

Directions:
1. Add the ingredients to bread machine pan in the order listed above, (except yeast) ; be sure to add the cheese with the flour.
2. Make a well in the flour; pour the yeast into the hole.
3. Select Basic bread cycle, medium crust color, and press Start.
4. When finished, transfer to a cooling rack for 10 minutes and serve warm.

Nutrition Info: Calories: 171, Sodium: 266 mg, Dietary Fiber: 0.9 g, Fat: 3.9 g, Carbs: 26.8 g, Protein: 6.7 g.

Pumpernickel Bread

Servings: 1 Loaf
Ingredients:
- 16 slice bread (2 pounds)
- 1 1/3 cups water, lukewarm between 80 and 90^{0}F
- 2 large eggs, room temperature and not cold
- ¼ cup oil
- ¼ cup honey
- 3 tablespoons dry milk powder

- ¼ cup cocoa powder
- 3 tablespoons caraway seeds
- 1 tablespoon instant coffee granules
- 2 teaspoons table salt
- 1 cup rye flour
- 1 cup whole wheat bread flour
- 2 cups white bread flour
- 2 ¼ teaspoons bread machine yeast
- 12 slice bread (1 ½ pounds)
- 3/4 cups water, lukewarm between 80 and 90°F
- 2 large eggs, room temperature and not cold
- 2 tablespoons oil
- 2 tablespoons honey
- 3 tablespoons dry milk powder
- 3 tablespoons cocoa powder
- 2 tablespoons caraway seeds
- 2 teaspoon instant coffee granules
- 1 1/2 teaspoons table salt
- 3/4 cup rye flour
- 3/4 cup whole wheat bread flour
- 1 1/2 cups white bread flour
- 1 3/4 teaspoons bread machine yeast

Directions:

1. Choose the size of loaf you would like to make and measure your ingredients. If you want to make a 1-pound or 2 ½-pound loaf, please adjust your ingredient quantities accordingly. You can look at the conversion table at the end of the book for easy adjustments or click here.
2. Take the bread pan; add the ingredients in order listed above.
3. Secure the pan into the bread machine and close the lid.
4. Power the bread maker and select the option of the bread – White/Basic – then the size of the loaf you are making, and finally the crust color you desire. Start the machine.
5. After the bread cycle is done and the bread is cooked, carefully remove the pan from the machine. Use a potholder as the handle will be very hot. Let rest for a few minutes.
6. Remove the bread from the pan and allow to cool down on a wired rack for at least 10 minutes or more before slicing.

Nutrition Info: (Per Serving):Calories 134, fat 3.1 g, carbs 19 g, sodium 143 mg, protein 4.2 g

Rosemary Focaccia Bread

Servings: 4 - 6
Cooking Time: 3 Hours

Ingredients:

- 1 cup, plus 3 tablespoons water
- 1 tablespoon extra-virgin olive oil
- 1 teaspoon salt
- 2 teaspoons fresh rosemary, chopped
- 3 cups bread flour
- 1 1/2 teaspoons instant yeast

- For the topping:
- 3 tablespoons olive oil
- Coarse salt
- Red pepper flakes

Directions:
1. Add water, oil, salt, rosemary, and flour to the bread maker pan.
2. Make a well in the center of the dry ingredients and add the yeast.
3. Select Dough cycle and press Start.
4. Transfer finished dough to a floured surface.
5. Cover and let rest for 5 minutes.
6. Form dough into a smooth ball and roll into a 12-inch round.
7. Place on a 12-inch pizza pan that has been lightly greased with olive oil. Poke dough randomly with fingertips to form dimples. Brush top with olive oil and sprinkle with salt and red pepper flakes to taste.
8. Let rise uncovered in warm, draft-free space for about 30 minutes.
9. Bake at 425°F for 18 to 22 minutes or until done.
10. Serve warm.

Nutrition Info: Calories: 312, Sodium: 390 mg, Dietary Fiber: 2.1 g, Fat: 10.1 g, Carbs: 48.3 g, Protein: 6.9 g.

Multigrain Honey Bread

Servings: 1 Loaf

Ingredients:
- 16 slice bread (2 pounds)
- 1½ cups lukewarm water
- 2 tablespoons unsalted butter, melted
- 1 tablespoon honey
- 1 teaspoon table salt
- 1½ cups multigrain flour
- 2¾ cups white bread flour
- 2 teaspoons bread machine yeast
- 12 slice bread (1½ pounds)
- 1⅛ cups lukewarm water
- 2 tablespoons unsalted butter, melted
- 1½ tablespoons honey
- 1½ teaspoons table salt
- 1⅛ cups multigrain flour
- 2 cups white bread flour
- 1½ teaspoons bread machine yeast

Directions:
1. Choose the size of loaf you would like to make and measure your ingredients.
2. Add the ingredients to the bread pan in the order listed above.
3. Place the pan in the bread machine and close the lid.
4. Turn on the bread maker. Select the White/Basic setting, then the loaf size, and finally the crust color. Start the cycle.

5. When the cycle is finished and the bread is baked, carefully remove the pan from the machine. Use a potholder as the handle will be very hot. Let rest for a few minutes.
6. Remove the bread from the pan and allow to cool on a wire rack for at least 10 minutes before slicing.
Nutrition Info: (Per Serving):Calories 144, fat 2.2 g, carbs 26.3 g, sodium 287 mg, protein 4.1 g

Insane Coffee Cake

Servings: 10 - 12
Cooking Time: 2 Hours
Ingredients:
- 7/8 cup of milk
- 1/4 cup of sugar
- 1 teaspoon salt
- 1 egg yolk
- 1 tablespoon butter
- 2 1/4 cups bread flour
- 2 teaspoons of active dry yeast
- For the topping:
- 2 tablespoons butter, melted
- 2 tablespoons brown sugar
- 1 teaspoon cinnamon

Directions:
1. Set the topping ingredients aside and add the rest of the ingredients to the bread pan in the order above.
2. Set the bread machine to the Dough cycle.
3. Butter a 9-by-9-inch glass baking dish and pour the dough into the dish. Cover with a towel and let rise for about 10 minutes.
4. Preheat an oven to 375°F.
5. Brush the dough with the melted butter.
6. Mix the brown sugar and cinnamon in a bowl and sprinkle on top of the coffee cake.
7. Let the topped dough rise, uncovered, for another 30 minutes.
8. Place in oven and bake for 30 to 35 minutes or until a wooden toothpick inserted into the center comes out clean and dry.
9. When baked, let the coffee cake rest for 10 minutes. Carefully remove the coffee cake from the dish with a rubber spatula, slice and serve.
Nutrition Info: Calories: 148, Sodium: 211 mg, Dietary Fiber: 0.9 g, Fat: 3.9 g, Carbs: 24.9 g, Protein: 3.5 g.

Quinoa Oatmeal Bread

Servings: 6
Cooking Time: 3 Hours And 48 Minutes
Ingredients:
- Quinoa flakes – ½ cup
- Buttermilk – 1 cup
- Salt – 1 tsp.

- Sugar – 1 tbsp.
- Honey – 1 tbsp.
- Unsalted butter – 4 tbsp.
- Quick-cooking oats – ½ cup
- Whole wheat flour – ½ cup
- Bread flour – 1 ½ cups
- Yeast – 1 ½ tsp.

Directions:
1. Add everything according to the bread machine instructions.
2. Select Whole Grain and bake.
3. Remove the bread when done.
4. Cool, slice, and serve.

Nutrition Info: (Per Serving): Calories: 295; Total Fat: 14 g; Saturated Fat: 7 g; Carbohydrates: 37 g; Cholesterol: 25 mg; Fiber: 4 g; Calcium: 119 mg; Sodium: 517 mg; Protein: 6 g

Basic Bulgur Bread

Servings: 1 Loaf

Ingredients:
- 16 slice bread (2 pounds)
- ½ cup lukewarm water
- ½ cup bulgur wheat
- 1⅓ cups lukewarm milk
- 1⅓ tablespoons unsalted butter, melted
- 1⅓ tablespoons sugar
- 1 teaspoon table salt
- 4 cups bread flour
- 2 teaspoons bread machine yeast
- 12 slice bread (1½ pounds)
- ⅓ cup lukewarm water
- ⅓ cup bulgur wheat
- 1 cup lukewarm milk
- 1 tablespoon unsalted butter, melted
- 1 tablespoon sugar
- ¾ teaspoon table salt
- 3 cups bread flour
- 1½ teaspoons bread machine yeast

Directions:
1. Choose the size of loaf you would like to make and measure your ingredients.
2. Add the water and bulgur wheat to the bread pan and set aside for 25–30 minutes for the bulgur wheat to soften.
3. Add the other ingredients to the bread pan in the order listed above.
4. Place the pan in the bread machine and close the lid.
5. Turn on the bread maker. Select the White/Basic setting, then the loaf size, and finally the crust color. Start the cycle.
6. When the cycle is finished and the bread is baked, carefully remove the pan from the machine. Use a potholder as the handle will be very hot. Let rest for a few minutes.

7. Remove the bread from the pan and allow to cool on a wire rack for at least 10 minutes before slicing.

Nutrition Info: (Per Serving):Calories 160, fat 2.6 g, carbs 28.7 g, sodium 163 mg, protein 5 g

Whole Wheat Corn Bread

Servings: 1 Loaf

Ingredients:
- 16 slice bread (2 pounds)
- 1⅓ cups lukewarm water
- 2 tablespoons light brown sugar
- 1 large egg, beaten
- 2 tablespoons unsalted butter, melted
- 1½ teaspoons table salt
- ¾ cup whole wheat flour
- ¾ cup cornmeal
- 2¾ cups white bread flour
- 2½ teaspoons bread machine yeast
- 12 slice bread (1½ pounds)
- 1 cup lukewarm water
- 1½ tablespoons light brown sugar
- 1 medium egg, beaten
- 1½ tablespoons unsalted butter, melted
- 1½ teaspoons table salt
- ½ cup whole wheat flour
- ½ cup cornmeal
- 2 cups white bread flour
- 1½ teaspoons bread machine yeast

Directions:
1. Choose the size of loaf you would like to make and measure your ingredients.
2. Add the ingredients to the bread pan in the order listed above.
3. Place the pan in the bread machine and close the lid.
4. Turn on the bread maker. Select the White/Basic setting, then the loaf size, and finally the crust color. Start the cycle.
5. When the cycle is finished and the bread is baked, carefully remove the pan from the machine. Use a potholder as the handle will be very hot. Let rest for a few minutes.
6. Remove the bread from the pan and allow to cool on a wire rack for at least 10 minutes before slicing.

Nutrition Info: (Per Serving):Calories 146, fat 5.7 g, carbs 19.3 g, sodium 124 mg, protein 4.8 g

French Bread

Servings: 8
Cooking Time: 3 Hours And 35 Minutes

Ingredients:
- Water - ⅔ cup
- Olive oil - 2 tsp.

- Sugar - 1 tbsp.
- Salt - ⅔ tsp.
- White bread flour - 2 cups
- Bread machine or instant yeast - 1 tsp.

Directions:
1. Place everything in the bread machine according to machine recommendation.
2. Press French bread and Light or Medium crust. Press Start.
3. Remove the loaf from the machine and cool.
4. Slice and serve.

Nutrition Info: (Per Serving): Calories: 135; Total Fat: 2 g; Saturated Fat: 0 g; Carbohydrates: 26 g; Cholesterol: 13 mg; Fiber: 1 g; Calcium: 17 mg; Sodium: 245 mg; Protein: 3 g

Chocolate Coffee Bread

Servings: 14 Slices
Cooking Time: 3 H.

Ingredients:
- 1⅓ cups water
- ⅓ cup cocoa powder
- 1⅓ cups bread flour
- 1⅓ cups whole wheat flour
- 3 Tbsp powdered milk
- ½ tsp salt
- 1½ Tbsp honey
- 2 envelopes instant mocha cappuccino mix
- 2¼ tsp active dry yeast
- ½ cup semi-sweet chocolate chips

Directions:
1. Add each ingredient except chips and mocha mix to the bread machine in the order and at the temperature recommended by your bread machine manufacturer.
2. Close the lid, select the sweet loaf, low crust setting on your bread machine, and press start.
3. Add the chocolate chips and mocha mix about 5 minutes before the kneading cycle has finished.
4. When the bread machine has finished baking, remove the bread and put it on a cooling rack.

Wheat Bran Bread

Servings: 1 Loaf

Ingredients:
- 16 slice bread (2 pounds)
- 1½ cups lukewarm milk
- 3 tablespoons unsalted butter, melted
- ¼ cup sugar
- 2 teaspoons table salt
- ½ cup wheat bran
- 3½ cups white bread flour
- 2 teaspoons bread machine yeast

- 12 slice bread (1½ pounds)
- 1⅛ cups lukewarm milk
- 2¼ tablespoons unsalted butter, melted
- 3 tablespoons sugar
- 1½ teaspoons table salt
- ⅓ cup wheat bran
- 2⅔ cups white bread flour
- 1½ teaspoons bread machine yeast

Directions:
1. Choose the size of loaf you would like to make and measure your ingredients.
2. Add the ingredients to the bread pan in the order listed above.
3. Place the pan in the bread machine and close the lid.
4. Turn on the bread maker. Select the White/Basic setting, then the loaf size, and finally the crust color. Start the cycle.
5. When the cycle is finished and the bread is baked, carefully remove the pan from the machine. Use a potholder as the handle will be very hot. Let rest for a few minutes.
6. Remove the bread from the pan and allow to cool on a wire rack for at least 10 minutes before slicing.

Nutrition Info: (Per Serving):Calories 147, fat 2.8 g, carbs 24.6 g, sodium 312 mg, protein 3.8 g

Sunflower And Flax Seed Bread

Servings: 15
Cooking Time: 3 Hours And 25 Minutes
Ingredients:
- Water – 1 1/3 cups
- Butter – 2 tbsp., softened
- Honey – 3 tbsp.
- Bread flour – 1 ½ cups
- Whole wheat bread flour – 1 1/3 cups
- Salt – 1 tsp.
- Active dry yeast – 1 tsp.
- Flax seeds – ½ cup
- Sunflower seeds – ½ cup

Directions:
1. Place everything (except sunflower seeds) in the bread machine according to machine recommendation.
2. Select Basic White cycle and press Start.
3. Add the seeds after the alert sounds.
4. Cool, slice, and serve.

Nutrition Info: (Per Serving): Calories: 140.3; Total Fat: 4.2 g; Saturated Fat: 1.2 g; Carbohydrates: 22.7 g; Cholesterol: 4.1 mg; Fiber: 3.1 g; Calcium: 19.8 mg; Sodium: 168.6 mg; Protein: 4.2 g

Basic Seed Bread

Servings: 1 Loaf

Ingredients:

- 16 slice bread (2 pounds)
- 1½ cups lukewarm water
- 2 tablespoons unsalted butter, melted
- 2 tablespoons sugar
- 1½ teaspoons table salt
- 3¼ cups white bread flour
- ¾ cup ground chia seeds
- 2 tablespoons sesame seeds
- 2 teaspoons bread machine yeast
- 12 slice bread (1½ pounds)
- 1⅛ cups lukewarm water
- 1½ tablespoons unsalted butter, melted
- 1½ tablespoons sugar
- 1⅛ teaspoons table salt
- 2½ cups white bread flour
- ½ cup ground chia seeds
- 1½ tablespoons sesame seeds
- 1½ teaspoons bread machine yeast

Directions:

1. Choose the size of loaf you would like to make and measure your ingredients.
2. Add the ingredients to the bread pan in the order listed above.
3. Place the pan in the bread machine and close the lid.
4. Turn on the bread maker. Select the White/Basic setting, then the loaf size, and finally the crust color. Start the cycle.
5. When the cycle is finished and the bread is baked, carefully remove the pan from the machine. Use a potholder as the handle will be very hot. Let rest for a few minutes.
6. Remove the bread from the pan and allow to cool on a wire rack for at least 10 minutes before slicing.

Nutrition Info: (Per Serving):Calories 153, fat 2.3 g, carbs 24.8 g, sodium 208 mg, protein 5.3 g

Lemon Cake

Servings: 12
Cooking Time: 2 Hours 50 Minutes

Ingredients:

- 3 large eggs, beaten
- 1/3 cup 2% milk
- 1/2 cup butter, melted
- 2 cups all-purpose flour
- 3 teaspoons baking powder
- 1 1/3 cup sugar
- 1 teaspoon vanilla extract
- 2 lemons, zested
- For the glaze:
- 1 cup powdered sugar
- 2 tablespoons lemon juice, freshly squeezed

Directions:
1.   Prepare the glaze by whisking the powdered sugar and lemon juice together in a small mixing bowl and set aside.
2.   Add all of the remaining ingredients to the baking pan in the order listed.
3.   Select the Sweet bread, medium color crust, and press Start.
4.   When baked, transfer the baking pan to a cooling rack.
5.   When the cake has cooled completely, gently shake the cake out onto a serving plate. Glaze the cool cake and serve.

Nutrition Info: Calories: 290, Sodium: 77 mg, Dietary Fiber: 0.6 g, Fat: 9.3 g, Carbs: 42.9 g, Protein: 4 g.

Parsley And Chive Pull-apart Rolls

Servings: 16
Cooking Time: 3 Hours
Ingredients:
- 1 cup buttermilk
- 6 tablespoons unsalted butter, cut into 6 pieces
- 3 2/3 cups all-purpose flour
- 2 1/4 teaspoons instant yeast
- 1/3 cup granulated sugar
- 1 teaspoon salt
- 3 large egg yolks
- 1/4 cup chives, chopped
- 1/4 cup parsley, chopped
- For the topping:
- 1/4 cup butter, melted

Directions:
1.   Combine the buttermilk and the 6 tablespoons butter in a small saucepan and warm until the butter melts, stirring continuously. Add the packet of instant yeast and allow to stand for five minutes.
2.   Mix the egg yolks with a fork and add to the above mixture and blend.
3.   Combine the flour, sugar, salt and herbs.
4.   Add first the wet then the dry ingredients to your bread machine.
5.   Set on Dough cycle and press Start.
6.   Lightly grease a 9-by-13-inch glass baking dish.
7.   Turn the dough out onto a clean work surface and press down gently. If the dough is too sticky add a little flour to the work surface. Using a bench scraper or a chef's knife, divide the dough into 16 equal pieces
8.   Work one piece of dough at a time into a ball; keep the others covered with plastic wrap until ready to bake.
9.   Cover the entire baking dish with plastic wrap and let the balls rise in a warm space, about 40 to 60 minutes.
10. Preheat an oven to 375°F and bake 20 to 25 minutes, or until lightly golden brown.
11. Remove from the oven and brush the tops with melted butter, serve warm.

Nutrition Info: Calories: 196, Sodium: 201 mg, Dietary Fiber: 0.9 g, Fat: 8.4 g, Carbs: 26.5 g, Protein: 3.8 g.

Honey Wheat Bread

Servings: 1 Loaf
Ingredients:
- 16 slice bread (2 pounds)
- 1⅔ cups boiling water
- ¼ cup + 4 teaspoons cracked wheat
- ¼ cup + 4 teaspoons unsalted butter, melted
- ¼ cup honey
- 2 teaspoons table salt
- 1⅓ cups whole-wheat flour
- 2⅔ cups white bread flour
- 2½ teaspoons bread machine yeast
- 12 slice bread (1½ pounds)
- 1¼ cups boiling water
- ¼ cup cracked wheat
- ¼ cup unsalted butter, melted
- 3 tablespoons honey
- 1½ teaspoons table salt
- 1 cup whole-wheat flour
- 2 cups white bread flour
- 2 teaspoons bread machine yeast

Directions:
1. Choose the size of loaf you would like to make and measure your ingredients.
2. Add the boiling water and cracked wheat to the bread pan; set aside for 25–30 minutes for the wheat to soften.
3. Add the other ingredients to the bread pan in the order listed above.
4. Place the pan in the bread machine and close the lid.
5. Turn on the bread maker. Select the White/Basic setting, then the loaf size, and finally the crust color. Start the cycle.
6. When the cycle is finished and the bread is baked, carefully remove the pan from the machine. Use a potholder as the handle will be very hot. Let rest for a few minutes.
7. Remove the bread from the pan and allow to cool on a wire rack for at least 10 minutes before slicing.
Nutrition Info: (Per Serving):Calories 168, fat 4.3 g, carbs 31.3 g, sodium 296 mg, protein 4.1 g

Pizza Dough

Servings: 12 - 14
Cooking Time: 1 Hour 30 Minutes
Ingredients:
- 1 1/4 cups water
- 3 cups bread flour
- 1 teaspoon milk powder
- 1 tablespoon sugar
- 1 teaspoon salt
- 1 tablespoon yeast

Directions:

1. Add ingredients to the bread maker pan in the order listed above.
2. Select Dough cycle and press Start.
3. When finished, prepare dough by rolling it out in a pizza pan about to a 1-inch thickness.
4. Top with your favorite sauce, then cheese, then other toppings like pepperoni or veggies.
5. Bake at 425°F for 15 to 20 minutes or until crust is golden on the edges.
6. Enjoy hot!

Nutrition Info: Calories: 103, Sodium: 168 mg, Dietary Fiber: 0.9 g, Fat: 0.3 g, Carbs: 21.7 g, Protein: 3.1 g.

Three-seed Bread

Servings: 8
Cooking Time: 3 Hours And 25 Minutes
Ingredients:
- Water – 2/3 cup plus 2 tsp.
- Butter – 1 tbsp., softened
- Honey – 1 tbsp.
- Sunflower seeds – 2 tbsp.
- Sesame seeds – 2 tbsp.
- Poppy seeds – 2 tbsp.
- Salt – ¾ tsp.
- Whole wheat flour – 1 cup
- Bread flour - 1 cup
- Nonfat dry milk powder – 3 tbsp.
- Active dry yeast – 2 tsp.

Directions:
1. Put all ingredients in the bread machine pan according to its order.
2. Select Basic bread and press Start.
3. Remove the bread when done.
4. Cool, slice, and serve.

Nutrition Info: (Per Serving): Calories: 84; Total Fat: 2 g; Saturated Fat: 1 g; Carbohydrates: 14 g; Cholesterol: 2 mg; Fiber: 1 g; Calcium: 22 mg; Sodium: 133 mg; Protein: 3 g

Sausage Herb And Onion Bread

Servings: 14 Slices
Cooking Time: 3 H. 10 Min.
Ingredients:
- ¾ tsp basil leaves
- 1½ Tbsp sugar
- ⅜ cup wheat bran
- 1 medium onion, minced
- 2¼ tsp yeast
- ¾ tsp rosemary leaves
- ½ Tbsp salt
- 1½ Tbsp parmesan, grated
- 3 cups bread flour

- ¾ tsp oregano leaves
- ¾ tsp thyme leaves
- 1⅛ cups water
- ¾ cup Italian sausage

Directions:
1. Remove casing from sausage. Crumble the meat into a medium nonstick skillet.
2. Cook on medium heat, stirring and breaking up sausage until it begins to render its juices.
3. Add onion and cook for 2-3 minuts until it softens and the sausage is no longer pink.
4. Remove from heat and let it cool.
5. Add each ingredient to the bread machine in the order and at the temperature recommended by your bread machine manufacturer.
6. Close the lid, select the basic bread, medium crust setting on your bread machine, and press start.
7. When the bread machine has finished baking, remove the bread and put it on a cooling rack.

Fat-free Whole Wheat Bread

Servings: 12
Cooking Time: 1 Hour And 20 Minutes
Ingredients:
- Water – 1 7/8 cup
- White whole wheat flour – 4 2/3 cups
- Vital wheat gluten – 4 tbsp.
- Sugar – 2 tbsp.
- Salt – 1 ½ tsp.
- Rapid rise yeast – 2 ½ tsp.

Directions:
1. Add the water in the bread machine pan.
2. Add the remaining ingredients according to bread machine recommendation.
3. Choose Quick-Bake Whole Wheat cycle and press Start.
4. Remove the bread when complete.
5. Cool, slice, and serve.

Nutrition Info: (Per Serving): Calories: 134; Total Fat: 0.6 g; Saturated Fat: 0 g; Carbohydrates: 27.6 g; Cholesterol: 11 mg; Fiber: 6.5 g; Calcium: 18 mg; Sodium: 221.5 mg; Protein: 6.5 g

Italian Easter Cake

Servings: 4 Slices
Cooking Time: 3 H.
Ingredients:
- 1¾ cups wheat flour
- 2½ Tbsp quick-acting dry yeast
- 8 Tbsp sugar
- ½ tsp salt
- 3 chicken eggs
- ¾ cup milk
- 3 Tbsp butter

- 1 cup raisins

Directions:
1. Add each ingredient except the raisins to the bread machine in the order and at the temperature recommended by your bread machine manufacturer.
2. Close the lid, select the sweet loaf, low crust setting on your bread machine, and press start.
3. When the dough is kneading, add the raisins.
4. When the bread machine has finished baking, remove the bread and put it on a cooling rack.

Buttermilk Bread

Servings: 1 Loaf

Ingredients:
- 16 slice bread (2 pounds)
- 1¼ cups lukewarm buttermilk
- 2 tablespoons unsalted butter, melted
- 2 tablespoons sugar
- 1½ teaspoons table salt
- ½ teaspoon baking powder
- 3½ cups white bread flour
- 2¼ teaspoons bread machine yeast
- 12 slice bread (1½ pounds)
- 1¼ cups lukewarm buttermilk
- 1½ tablespoons unsalted butter, melted
- 1½ tablespoons sugar
- 1⅛ teaspoons table salt
- ⅓ teaspoon baking powder
- 2⅔ cups white bread flour
- 1⅔ teaspoons bread machine yeast

Directions:
1. Choose the size of loaf you would like to make and measure your ingredients.
2. Add the ingredients to the bread pan in the order listed above.
3. Place the pan in the bread machine and close the lid.
4. Turn on the bread maker. Select the White/Basic setting, then the loaf size, and finally the crust color. Start the cycle.
5. When the cycle is finished and the bread is baked, carefully remove the pan from the machine. Use a potholder as the handle will be very hot. Let rest for a few minutes.
6. Remove the bread from the pan and allow to cool on a wire rack for at least 10 minutes before slicing.

Nutrition Info: (Per Serving):Calories 132, fat 2.2 g, carbs 23.4 g, sodium 234 mg, protein 4.3 g

Banana Chocolate Chip Bread

Servings: 14 Slices
Cooking Time: 2 H.

Ingredients:
- 2 eggs
- ⅓ cup melted butter

- ⅛ cup milk
- 2 mashed bananas
- 2 cups all-purpose bread flour
- ⅔ cup sugar
- 1¼ tsp baking powder
- ½ tsp baking soda
- ½ tsp salt
- ½ cup chopped walnuts
- ½ cup chocolate chips

Directions:
1. Add each ingredient to the bread machine in the order and at the temperature recommended by your bread machine manufacturer.
2. Close the lid, select the quick bread, low crust setting on your bread machine, and press start.
3. When the bread machine has finished baking, remove the bread and put it on a cooling rack.

Cinnamon Rolls

Servings: 12 Rolls
Cooking Time: 2 H.
Ingredients:
- For the cinnamon roll dough:
- 1 cup milk
- 1 large egg
- 4 Tbsp butter
- 3⅓ cups bread flour
- 3 Tbsp sugar
- ½ tsp salt
- 2 tsp active dry yeast
- For the filling:
- ¼ cup butter, melted
- ¼ cup sugar
- 2 tsp cinnamon
- ½ tsp nutmeg
- ⅓ cup nuts, chopped and toasted
- For the icing:
- 1 cup powdered sugar
- 1 - 2 Tbsp milk
- ½ tsp vanilla

Directions:
1. Add each ingredient to the bread machine in the order and at the temperature recommended by your bread machine manufacturer.
2. Select the dough cycle and press start.
3. When it's done, transfer the dough onto a floured surface.
4. Knead it for 1 minute, then let it rest for the next 15 minutes.
5. Roll out a rectangle. Spread ¼ cup of melted butter over the dough.
6. Sprinkle the dough with cinnamon, ¼ cup sugar, nutmeg, and nuts.

7. Roll the dough, beginning from a long side. Seal the edges and form an evenly shaped roll. Cut it into 1-inch pieces.
8. Put them on a greased baking pan.
9. Cover with towel and leave for 45 minutes to rise.
10. Bake at 375°F in a preheated oven for 20-25 minutes.
11. Remove from the oven. Cool for 10 minutes.
12. Mix the icing ingredients in a bowl. Adjust with sugar or milk to desired thickness.
13. Cover the rolls with icing and serve.

Citrus And Walnut Bread

Servings: 14 Slices
Cooking Time: 3 H.
Ingredients:
- ¾ cup lemon yogurt
- ½ cup orange juice
- 5 tsp caster sugar
- 1 tsp salt
- 2.5 Tbsp butter
- 2 cups unbleached white bread flour
- 1½ tsp easy blend dried yeast
- ⅓ cup chopped walnuts
- 2 tsp grated lemon rind
- 2 tsp grated orange rind

Directions:
1. Add each ingredient except the walnuts and orange and lemon rind to the bread machine one by one, as per the manufacturer's instructions.
2. Close the lid, select the basic bread, medium crust setting on your bread machine, and press start.
3. Add the walnuts, and orange and lemon rind during the 2nd kneading cycle:
4. When the bread machine has finished baking, remove the bread and put it on a cooling rack.

White Bread

Servings: 8
Cooking Time: 3 Hours And 25 Minutes
Ingredients:
- Water - ¾ cup
- Melted butter - 1 tbsp., cooled
- Sugar - 1 tbsp.
- Salt - ¾ tsp.
- Skim milk powder - 2 tbsp.
- White bread flour - 2 cups
- Bread machine or instant yeast - ¾ tsp.

Directions:
1. Add the ingredients according to the manufacturer's recommendation.
2. Press Basic/White bread. Choose Light or Medium crust, then press Start.

3. When done, remove the bucket from the machine.
4. Cool for 5 minutes.
5. Remove the bread from the bucket. Slice and serve.

Nutrition Info: (Per Serving): Calories: 140; Total Fat: 2 g; Saturated Fat: 1 g; Carbohydrates: 27 g; Cholesterol: 10 mg; Fiber: 1 g; Calcium: 7 mg; Sodium: 215 mg; Protein: 4 g

Oat Nut Bread

Servings: 14 Slices
Cooking Time: 3 H.
Ingredients:
- 1¼ cups water
- ½ cup quick oats
- ¼ cup brown sugar, firmly packed
- 1 Tbsp butter
- 1½ tsp salt
- 3 cups bread flour
- ¾ cup chopped walnuts
- 1 package dry bread yeast

Directions:
1. Add each ingredient to the bread machine in the order and at the temperature recommended by your bread machine manufacturer.
2. Close the lid, select the rapid rise, medium crust setting on your bread machine, and press start.
3. When the bread machine has finished baking, remove the bread and put it on a cooling rack.

Texas Roadhouse Rolls

Servings: 18 Rolls
Cooking Time: 20 Min.
Ingredients:
- ¼ cup warm water (80ºF - 90ºF
- 1 cup warm milk (80ºF -90ºF)
- 1 tsp salt
- 1½ Tbsp butter + more for brushing
- 1 egg
- ¼ cup sugar
- 3½ cups unbleached bread flour
- 1 envelope dry active yeast
- For Texas roadhouse cinnamon butter:
- ½ cup sweet, creamy salted butter, softened
- ⅓ cup confectioners' sugar
- 1 tsp ground cinnamon

Directions:
1. Add each ingredient to the bread machine in the order and at the temperature recommended by your bread machine manufacturer.
2. Select the dough cycle and press start.

3. Once cycle is done, transfer your dough onto a lightly floured surface.
4. Roll out the rectangle, fold it in half. Let it rest for 15 minutes.
5. Cut the roll into 18 squares. Transfer them onto a baking sheet.
6. Bake at 350°F in a preheated oven for 10-15 minutes.
7. Remove dough from the oven and brush the top with butter.
8. Beat the softened butter with a mixer to make it fluffy. Gradually add the sugar and cinnamon while blending. Mix well.
9. Take out the rolls, let them cool for 2-3 minutes.
10. Spread them with cinnamon butter on the top while they are warm.

SPICE, NUT & HERB BREAD

Cinnamon Milk Bread

Servings: 1 Loaf

Ingredients:
- 16 slice bread (2 pounds)
- 1⅔ cups lukewarm milk
- 1 egg, at room temperature
- ⅓ cup unsalted butter, melted
- ⅔ cup sugar
- ⅔ teaspoon table salt
- 4 cups white bread flour
- 2 teaspoons ground cinnamon
- 2¼ teaspoons bread machine yeast
- 12 slice bread (1½ pounds)
- 1 cup lukewarm milk
- 1 egg, at room temperature
- ¼ cup unsalted butter, melted
- ½ cup sugar
- ½ teaspoon table salt
- 3 cups white bread flour
- 1½ teaspoons ground cinnamon
- 2 teaspoons bread machine yeast

Directions:
1. Choose the size of loaf you would like to make and measure your ingredients.
2. Add the ingredients to the bread pan in the order listed above.
3. Place the pan in the bread machine and close the lid.
4. Turn on the bread maker. Select the White/Basic setting, then the loaf size, and finally the crust color. Start the cycle.
5. When the cycle is finished and the bread is baked, carefully remove the pan from the machine. Use a potholder as the handle will be very hot. Let rest for a few minutes.
6. Remove the bread from the pan and allow to cool on a wire rack for at least 10 minutes before slicing.

Nutrition Info: (Per Serving):Calories 187, fat 5.1 g, carbs 33.4 g, sodium 143 mg, protein 4.6 g

Healthy Basil Whole Wheat Bread

Servings: 10

Cooking Time: 2 Hours

Ingredients:
- Olive oil – 2 tbsps.
- Basil – 1 tbsp.
- Water – 1 1/3 cups
- Whole wheat flour – 4 cups
- Salt – 2 tsps.
- Sugar – 3 tbsps.
- Active dry yeast – 2 tsps.

Directions:

1.   Add olive oil and water to the bread pan. Add remaining ingredients except for yeast to the bread pan. Make a small hole into the flour with your finger and add yeast to the hole. Make sure yeast will not be mixed with any liquids. Select whole wheat setting then select light/medium crust and start. Once loaf is done, remove the loaf pan from the machine. Allow it to cool for 5 minutes. Slice and serve.

Classic Italian Herb Bread

Servings: 10
Cooking Time: 2 Hours
Ingredients:
- Active dry yeast – ¼ oz.
- Dried Italian seasoning – 4 tsps.
- Sugar – 3 tbsps.
- All-purpose flour – 4 cups
- Olive oil – 1/3 cup
- Water – 1 1/3 cups
- Salt – 2 tsps.

Directions:

1.   Add olive oil and water to the bread pan. Add remaining ingredients except for yeast to the bread pan. Make a small hole in the flour with your finger and add yeast to the hole. Make sure yeast will not be mixed with any liquids. Select basic setting then select light/medium crust and start. Once loaf is done, remove the loaf pan from the machine. Allow it to cool for 10 minutes. Slice and serve.

Pecan Raisin Bread

Servings: 1 Loaf
Cooking Time: 10 Minutes Plus Fermenting Time
Ingredients:
- 1 cup plus 2 Tbsp water (70°F to 80°F)
- 8 tsp butter
- 1 egg
- 6 Tbsp sugar
- ¼ cup nonfat dry milk powder
- 1 tsp salt
- 4 cups bread flour
- 1 Tbsp active dry yeast
- 1 cup finely chopped pecans
- 1 cup raisins

Directions:

1.   Preparing the Ingredients
2.   Add each ingredient to the bread machine except the pecans and raisins in the order and at the temperature recommended by your bread machine manufacturer.
3.   Select the Bake cycle

4. Close the lid, select the basic bread, medium crust setting on your bread machine, and press start.
5. Just before the final kneading, add the pecans and raisins.
6. When the bread machine has finished baking, remove the bread and put it on a cooling rack.

Oatmeal Sunflower Bread

Servings: 10
Cooking Time: 3 Hours 30 Minutes
Ingredients:
- Water – 1 cup.
- Honey – ¼ cup.
- Butter – 2 tbsps., softened
- Bread flour – 3 cups.
- Old fashioned oats – ½ cup.
- Milk powder – 2 tbsps.
- Salt – 1 ¼ tsps.
- Active dry yeast – 2 ¼ tsps.
- Sunflower seeds – ½ cup.

Directions:
1. Add all ingredients except for sunflower seeds into the bread machine pan. Select basic setting then select light/medium crust and press start. Add sunflower seeds just before the final kneading cycle. Once loaf is done, remove the loaf pan from the machine. Allow it to cool for 10 minutes. Slice and serve.

Whole Wheat Raisin Bread

Servings: 10
Cooking Time: 2 Hours
Ingredients:
- Whole wheat flour – 3 ½ cups
- Dry yeast – 2 tsps.
- Eggs – 2, lightly beaten
- Butter – ¼ cup, softened
- Water – ¾ cup
- Milk – 1/3 cup
- Salt – 1 tsp.
- Sugar – 1/3 cup
- Cinnamon – 4 tsps.
- Raisins – 1 cup

Directions:
1. Add water, milk, butter, and eggs to the bread pan. Add remaining ingredients except for yeast to the bread pan. Make a small hole into the flour with your finger and add yeast to the hole. Make sure yeast will not be mixed with any liquids. Select whole wheat setting then select light/medium crust and start. Once loaf is done, remove the loaf pan from the machine. Allow it to cool for 10 minutes. Slice and serve.

Pistachio Cherry Bread

Servings: 1 Loaf
Ingredients:
- 16 slice bread (2 pounds)
- 1⅛ cups lukewarm water
- 1 egg, at room temperature
- ¼ cup butter, softened
- ¼ cup packed dark brown sugar
- 1½ teaspoons table salt
- 3¾ cups white bread flour
- ½ teaspoon ground nutmeg
- Dash allspice
- 2 teaspoons bread machine yeast
- 1 cup dried cherries
- ½ cup unsalted pistachios, chopped
- 12 slice bread (1½ pounds)
- ¾ cup lukewarm water
- 1 egg, at room temperature
- 3 tablespoons butter, softened
- 3 tablespoons packed dark brown sugar
- 1⅛ teaspoons table salt
- 2¾ cups white bread flour
- ½ teaspoon ground nutmeg
- Dash allspice
- 1½ teaspoons bread machine yeast
- ¾ cup dried cherries
- ⅓ cup unsalted pistachios, chopped

Directions:
1. Choose the size of loaf you would like to make and measure your ingredients.
2. Add all of the ingredients except for the pistachios and cherries to the bread pan in the order listed above.
3. Place the pan in the bread machine and close the lid.
4. Turn on the bread maker. Select the White/Basic or Fruit/Nut (if your machine has this setting) setting, then the loaf size, and finally the crust color. Start the cycle.
5. When the machine signals to add ingredients, add the pistachios and cherries. (Some machines have a fruit/nut hopper where you can add the pistachios and cherries when you start the machine. The machine will automatically add them to the dough during the baking process.)
6. When the cycle is finished and the bread is baked, carefully remove the pan from the machine. Use a potholder as the handle will be very hot. Let rest for a few minutes.
7. Remove the bread from the pan and allow to cool on a wire rack for at least 10 minutes before slicing.
Nutrition Info: (Per Serving):Calories 196, fat 5.3 g, carbs 27.8 g, sodium 237 mg, protein 4.4 g

Herbed Pesto Bread

Servings: 1 Loaf
Cooking Time: 10 Minutes

Ingredients:
- 12 slices bread (1½ pounds)
- 1 cup water, at 80°F to 90°F
- 2¼ tablespoons melted butter, cooled
- 1½ teaspoons minced garlic
- ¾ tablespoon sugar
- 1 teaspoon salt
- 3 tablespoons chopped fresh parsley
- 1½ tablespoons chopped fresh basil
- ⅓ cup grated Parmesan cheese
- 3 cups white bread flour
- 1¼ teaspoons bread machine or active dry yeast

Directions:
1. Preparing the Ingredients.
2. Choose the size of loaf of your preference and then measure the ingredients.
3. Add all of the ingredients mentioned previously in the list.
4. Close the lid after placing the pan in the bread machine.
5. Select the Bake cycle
6. Turn on the bread machine. Select the White/Basic setting, select the loaf size, and the crust color. Press start.
7. When the cycle is finished, carefully remove the pan from the bread maker and let it rest.
8. Remove the bread from the pan, put in a wire rack to Cool about 10 minutes. Slice

Garlic, Herb, And Cheese Bread

Servings: One Loaf (12 Slices)
Cooking Time: 15 Minutes
Ingredients:
- 1/2 cup ghee
- Six eggs
- 2 cups almond flour
- 1 tbsp baking powder
- 1/2 tsp xanthan gum
- 1 cup cheddar cheese, shredded
- 1 tbsp garlic powder
- 1 tbsp parsley
- 1/2 tbsp oregano
- 1/2 tsp salt

Directions:
1. Lightly beat eggs and ghee before pouring into bread machine pan.
2. Add the remaining ingredients to the pan.
3. Set bread machine to gluten-free.
4. When the bread is finished, remove the bread pan from the bread machine.
5. Let it cool for a while before transferring into a cooling rack.
6. You can store your bread for up to 5 days in the refrigerator.

Nutrition Info: Calories: 156 ;Carbohydrates: 4g;Protein: 5g;Fat: 13g

Lavender Buttermilk Bread

Servings: 14 Slices
Cooking Time: 3 H.
Ingredients:
- ½ cup water
- ⅞ cup buttermilk
- ¼ cup olive oil
- 3 Tbsp finely chopped fresh lavender leaves
- 1 ¼ tsp finely chopped fresh lavender flowers
- Grated zest of 1 lemon
- 4 cups bread flour
- 2 tsp salt
- 2 ¾ tsp bread machine yeast

Directions:
1. Add each ingredient to the bread machine in the order and at the temperature recommended by your bread machine manufacturer.
2. Close the lid, select the basic bread, medium crust setting on your bread machine and press start.
3. When the bread machine has finished baking, remove the bread and put it on a cooling rack.

Molasses Candied-ginger Bread

Servings: 1 Loaf
Cooking Time: 10 Minutes
Ingredients:
- 12 slices bread (1½ pounds)
- 1 cup milk, at 80°F to 90°F
- 1 egg, at room temperature
- ¼ cup dark molasses
- 3 tablespoons butter, melted and cooled
- ½ teaspoon salt
- ¼ cup chopped candied ginger
- ½ cup quick oats
- 3 cups white bread flour
- 2 teaspoons bread machine or instant yeast

Directions:
1. Preparing the Ingredients.
2. Choose the size of loaf of your preference and then measure the ingredients.
3. Add all of the ingredients mentioned previously in the list.
4. Close the lid after placing the pan in the bread machine.
5. Select the Bake cycle
6. Turn on the bread machine. Select the White/Basic setting, select the loaf size, and the crust color. Press start.
7. When the cycle is finished, carefully remove the pan from the bread maker and let it rest.
8. Remove the bread from the pan, put in a wire rack to Cool about 5 minutes. Slice

Onion Bacon Bread

Servings: 22 Slices
Cooking Time: 1 Hour
Ingredients:
- 1 ½ cups lukewarm water (80 degrees F)
- Two tablespoons sugar
- Three teaspoons active dry yeast
- 4 ½ cups wheat flour
- One whole egg
- Two teaspoons kosher salt
- One tablespoon olive oil
- Three small onions, chopped and lightly toasted
- 1 cup bacon, chopped

Directions:
1. Prepare all of the ingredients for your bread and measuring means (a cup, a spoon, kitchen scales).
2. Carefully measure the ingredients into the pan, except the bacon and onion.
3. Place all of the ingredients into a bucket in the right order, following the manual for your bread machine.
4. Close the cover.
5. Select the program of your bread machine to BASIC and choose the crust colour to MEDIUM.
6. Press START.
7. After the machine beeps, add the onion and bacon.
8. Wait until the program completes.
9. When done, take the bucket out and let it cool for 5-10 minutes.
10. Shake the loaf from the pan and let cool for 30 minutes on a cooling rack.
11. Slice, serve and enjoy the taste of fragrant Homemade Bread.

Nutrition Info: Calories: 391 Cal;Fat: 9.7 g;Cholesterol: 38 g;Sodium: 960 mg;Carbohydrates: 59.9 g;Total Sugars 1.2g;Protein 3.4g;Potassium 43mg

Chive Bread

Servings: 14 Slices
Cooking Time: 3 H.
Ingredients:
- ⅔ cup milk (70°F to 80°F)
- ¼ cup water (70°F to 80°F)
- ¼ cup sour cream
- 2 Tbsp butter
- 1½ tsp sugar
- 1½ tsp salt
- 3 cups bread flour
- ⅛ tsp baking soda
- ¼ cup minced chives
- 2¼ tsp active dry yeast leaves

Directions:

1. Add each ingredient to the bread machine in the order and at the temperature recommended by your bread machine manufacturer.
2. Close the lid, select the basic bread, medium crust setting on your bread machine and press start.
3. When the bread machine has finished baking, remove the bread and put it on a cooling rack.

Coffee Raisin Bread

Servings: 10
Cooking Time: 3 Hours
Ingredients:
- Active dry yeast – 2 ½ tsps.
- Ground cloves – ¼ tsp.
- Ground allspice – ¼ tsp.
- Ground cinnamon – 1 tsp.
- Sugar – 3 tbsps.
- Egg – 1, lightly beaten
- Olive oil – 3 tbsps.
- Strong brewed coffee – 1 cup.
- Bread flour – 3 cups.
- Raisins – ¾ cup.
- Salt – 1 ½ tsps.

Directions:
1. Add all ingredients except for raisins into the bread machine pan. Select basic setting then select light/medium crust and press start. Add raisins just before the final kneading cycle. Once loaf is done, remove the loaf pan from the machine. Allow it to cool for 10 minutes. Slice and serve.

Chia Sesame Bread

Servings: 1 Loaf
Cooking Time: 10 Minutes
Ingredients:
- 12 slice bread (1½ pounds)
- 1 cup plus 2 tablespoons water, at 80°F to 90°F
- 1½ tablespoons melted butter, cooled
- 1½ tablespoons sugar
- 1⅛ teaspoons salt
- ½ cup ground chia seeds
- 1½ tablespoons sesame seeds
- 2½ cups white bread flour
- 1½ teaspoons bread machine or instant yeast

Directions:
1. Preparing the Ingredients.
2. Choose the size of loaf of your preference and then measure the ingredients.
3. Add all of the ingredients mentioned previously in the list.
4. Close the lid after placing the pan in the bread machine.

5. Select the Bake cycle
6. Turn on the bread machine. Select the White/Basic setting, select the loaf size, and the crust color. Press start.
7. When the cycle is finished, carefully remove the pan from the bread maker and let it rest.
8. Remove the bread from the pan, put in a wire rack to Cool about 5 minutes. Slice

Cheese Herb Bread

Servings: 10
Cooking Time: 3 Hours 27 Minutes
Ingredients:
- Active dry yeast – 1 ¼ tsps.
- Dried oregano – 1 ¼ tsps.
- Fennel seed – 1 ¼ tsps.
- Dried basil – 1 ¼ tsps.
- Asiago cheese – 2/3 cup, grated
- Bread flour – 3 ¼ cups
- Sugar – 1 tbsp.
- Salt – ¾ tsp.
- Water – 1 cup.

Directions:
1. Add all ingredients to the bread machine. Select sweet bread setting then select light/medium crust and start. Once loaf is done, remove the loaf pan from the machine. Allow it to cool for 10 minutes. Slice and serve.

Honey-spice Egg Bread

Servings: 1 Loaf
Cooking Time: 10 Minutes
Ingredients:
- 12 slices bread (1½ pounds)
- 1 cup milk, at 80°F to 90°F
- 2 eggs, at room temperature
- 1½ tablespoons melted butter, cooled
- 2 tablespoons honey
- 1 teaspoon salt
- 1 teaspoon ground cinnamon
- ½ teaspoon ground cardamom
- ½ teaspoon ground nutmeg
- 3 cups white bread flour
- 2 teaspoons bread machine or instant yeast

Directions:
1. Preparing the Ingredients.
2. Choose the size of loaf of your preference and then measure the ingredients.
3. Add all of the ingredients mentioned previously in the list.
4. Close the lid after placing the pan in the bread machine.
5. Select the Bake cycle

6. Turn on the bread machine. Select the White/Basic setting, select the loaf size, and the crust color. Press start.
7. When the cycle is finished, carefully remove the pan from the bread maker and let it rest.
8. Remove the bread from the pan, put in a wire rack to Cool about 10 minutes. Slice

Market Seed Bread

Servings: 1 Loaf
Cooking Time: 10 Minutes
Ingredients:
- 12 slice bread (1½ pounds)
- 1 cup plus 2 tablespoons milk, at 80°F to 90°F
- 1½ tablespoons melted butter, cooled
- 1½ tablespoons honey
- ¾ teaspoon salt
- 3 tablespoons flaxseed
- 3 tablespoons sesame seeds
- 1½ tablespoons poppy seeds
- 1¼ cups whole-wheat flour
- 1¾ cups white bread flour
- 1¾ teaspoons bread machine or instant yeast

Directions:
1. Preparing the Ingredients.
2. Choose the size of loaf of your preference and then measure the ingredients.
3. Add all of the ingredients mentioned previously in the list.
4. Close the lid after placing the pan in the bread machine.
5. Select the Bake cycle
6. Turn on the bread machine. Select the White/Basic setting, select the loaf size, and the crust color. Press start.
7. When the cycle is finished, carefully remove the pan from the bread maker and let it rest.
8. Remove the bread from the pan, put in a wire rack to Cool about 5 minutes. Slice

Aromatic Lavender Bread

Servings: 1 Loaf
Cooking Time: 10 Minutes
Ingredients:
- 16 slices bread (2 pounds)
- 1½ cups milk, at 80°F to 90°F
- 2 tablespoons melted butter, cooled
- 2 tablespoons sugar
- 2 teaspoons salt
- 2 teaspoons chopped fresh lavender flowers
- 1 teaspoon lemon zest
- ½ teaspoon chopped fresh thyme
- 4 cups white bread flour
- 1½ teaspoons bread machine or instant yeast

Directions:
1. Preparing the Ingredients.
2. Choose the size of loaf of your preference and then measure the ingredients.
3. Add all of the ingredients mentioned previously in the list.
4. Close the lid after placing the pan in the bread machine.
5. Select the Bake cycle
6. Turn on the bread machine. Select the White/Basic setting, select the loaf size, and the crust color. Press start.
7. When the cycle is finished, carefully remove the pan from the bread maker and let it rest.
8. Remove the bread from the pan, put in a wire rack to Cool about 10 minutes. Slice

Flaxseed Honey Bread

Servings: 1 Loaf
Cooking Time: 10 Minutes
Ingredients:
- 12 slices bread (1½ pounds)
- 1⅛ cups milk, at 80°F to 90°F
- 1½ tablespoons melted butter, cooled
- 1½ tablespoons honey
- 1 teaspoon salt
- ¼ cup flaxseed
- 3 cups white bread flour
- 1¼ teaspoons bread machine or instant yeast

Directions:
1. Preparing the Ingredients.
2. Choose the size of loaf of your preference and then measure the ingredients.
3. Add all of the ingredients mentioned previously in the list.
4. Close the lid after placing the pan in the bread machine.
5. Select the Bake cycle.
6. Turn on the bread machine. Select the White/Basic setting, select the loaf size, and the crust color. Press start.
7. When the cycle is finished, carefully remove the pan from the bread maker and let it rest.
8. Remove the bread from the pan, put in a wire rack to Cool about 5 minutes. Slice

Coco-cilantro Flatbread

Servings: 6 Pcs
Cooking Time: 15 Minutes
Ingredients:
- ½ cup Coconut Flour
- 2 tbsp. Flax Meal
- ¼ tsp Baking Soda
- pinch of Salt
- 1 tbsp. Coconut Oil
- 2 tbsp. Chopped Cilantro
- 1 cup Lukewarm Water

Directions:
1. Whisk together the coconut flour, flax, baking soda, and salt in a bowl.
2. Add in the water, coconut oil, and chopped cilantro.
3. Knead it until everything comes together into a smooth dough.
4. Leave to rest for about 15 minutes.
5. Divide the dough into six equal-sized portions.
6. Roll each of it into a ball, then flatten with a rolling pin in between sheets of parchment paper.
7. Refrigerate until ready to use.
8. To cook, heat in a non-stick pan for 2-3 minutes per side.

Nutrition Information:
- ;Kcal per serve 46;Fat: 4 g. (84%);Protein: 1 g. (3%);Carbs: 1 g. (13%)

Whole-wheat Seed Bread

Servings: 1 Loaf
Cooking Time: 10 Minutes
Ingredients:
- 12 slice bread (1½ pounds)
- 1⅛ cups water, at 80°F to 90°F
- 1½ tablespoons honey
- 1½ tablespoons melted butter, cooled
- ¾ teaspoon salt
- 2½ cups whole-wheat flour
- ¾ cup white bread flour
- 3 tablespoons raw sunflower seeds
- 1 tablespoon sesame seeds
- 1½ teaspoons bread machine or instant yeast

Directions:
1. Preparing the Ingredients.
2. Choose the size of loaf of your preference and then measure the ingredients.
3. Add all of the ingredients mentioned previously in the list.
4. Close the lid after placing the pan in the bread machine.
5. Select the Bake cycle
6. Turn on the bread machine. Select the Whole-Wheat/Whole-Grain bread, select the loaf size, and select light or medium crust. Press start.
7. When the cycle is finished, carefully remove the pan from the bread maker and let it rest.
8. Remove the bread from the pan, put in a wire rack to Cool about 5 minutes. Slice

Delicious Cranberry Bread

Servings: 10
Cooking Time: 3 Hours 27 Minutes
Ingredients:
- Warm water – 1 ½ cups
- Brown sugar – 2 tbsps.

- Salt – 1 ½ tsps.
- Olive oil – 2 tbsps.
- Flour – 4 cups
- Cinnamon – 1 ½ tsps.
- Cardamom – 1 ½ tsps.
- Dried cranberries – 1 cup
- Yeast – 2 tsps.

Directions:

1.   Add all ingredients to the bread machine in the listed order. Select sweet bread setting then select light/medium crust and start. Once loaf is done, remove the loaf pan from the machine. Allow it to cool for 20 minutes. Slice and serve.

Sunflower & Flax Seed Bread

Servings: 10
Cooking Time: 3 Hours
Ingredients:
- Water – 1 1/3 cups.
- Butter – 2 tbsps.
- Honey – 3 tbsps.
- Bread flour – 1 ½ cups.
- Whole wheat flour – 1 1/3 cups.
- Salt – 1 tsp.
- Active dry yeast – 1 tsp.
- Flax seeds – ½ cup.
- Sunflower seeds – ½ cup.

Directions:

1.   Add all ingredients except for sunflower seeds into the bread machine pan. Select basic setting then select light/medium crust and press start. Add sunflower seeds just before the final kneading cycle. Once loaf is done, remove the loaf pan from the machine. Allow it to cool for 10 minutes. Slice and serve.

Spiced Raisin Bread

Servings: 24
Cooking Time: 3 Hours And 25 Minutes
Ingredients:
- Water – 1 cup, plus 2 tbsp.
- Raisins – ¾ cup
- Butter – 2 tbsp., softened
- Brown sugar – 2 tbsp.
- Ground cinnamon – 2 tsp.
- Salt – 1 tsp.
- Ground nutmeg – ¼ tsp.
- Ground cloves – ¼ tsp.
- Orange zest – ¼ tsp., grated
- Bread flour – 3 cups

- Active dry yeast – 2 ¼ tsp.

Directions:
1. Put all ingredients in the bread machine pan according to its order.
2. Select Basic cycle and choose crust. Press Start.
3. When the bread is done, remove it.
4. Cool, slice, and serve.

Nutrition Info: (Per Serving): Calories: 78; Total Fat: 1 g; Saturated Fat: 1 g; Carbohydrates: 4 g; Cholesterol: 3 mg; Fiber: 1 g; Calcium: 7 mg; Sodium: 106 mg; Protein: 2 g

Pumpkin Coconut Almond Bread

Servings: 12 Slices
Cooking Time: 5 Minutes
Ingredients:
- 1/3 cup vegetable oil
- 3 large eggs
- 1 1/2 cups canned pumpkin puree
- 1 cup sugar
- 1 1/2 teaspoons baking powder
- 1/2 teaspoon baking soda
- 1/4 teaspoon salt
- 1 tablespoon allspice
- 3 cups all-purpose flour
- 1/2 cup coconut flakes, plus a small handful for the topping
- 2/3 cup slivered almonds, plus a tablespoonful for the topping
- Non-stick cooking spray

Directions:
1. Preparing the Ingredients
2. Spray bread maker pan with non-stick cooking spray. Mix oil, eggs, and pumpkin in a large mixing bowl.
3. Mix remaining ingredients together in a separate mixing bowl. Add wet ingredients to bread maker pan, and dry ingredients on top.
4. Select the Bake cycle
5. Select Dough cycle and press Start. Open lid and sprinkle top of bread with reserved coconut and almonds.
6. Set to Rapid for 1 hour 30 minutes and bake. Cool for 10 minutes on a wire rack before serving.

Anise Lemon Bread

Servings: 1 Loaf
Cooking Time: 10 Minutes
Ingredients:
- 12 slice bread (1½ pounds)
- ¾ cup water, at 80°F to 90°F
- 1 egg, at room temperature
- ¼ cup butter, melted and cooled

- ¼ cup honey
- ½ teaspoon salt
- 1 teaspoon anise seed
- 1 teaspoon lemon zest
- 3 cups white bread flour
- 2 teaspoons bread machine or instant yeast

Directions:
1. Preparing the Ingredients.
2. Choose the size of loaf of your preference and then measure the ingredients.
3. Add all of the ingredients mentioned previously in the list.
4. Close the lid after placing the pan in the bread machine.
5. Select the Bake cycle
6. Turn on the bread machine. Select the White/Basic setting, select the loaf size, and the crust color. Press start.
7. When the cycle is finished, carefully remove the pan from the bread maker and let it rest.
8. Remove the bread from the pan, put in a wire rack to Cool about 10 minutes. Slice

Herb Bread

Servings: 12
Cooking Time: 3 Hours And 25 Minutes
Ingredients:
- Water – 1 cup, plus 2 tbsp.
- Butter – 2 tbsp., softened
- Bread flour – 3 cups
- Fresh sage leaves – 2 tsp., chopped
- Fresh basil leaves – 1 tbsp., chopped
- Fresh oregano leaves – 1 tbsp., chopped
- Fresh thyme leaves – 2 tsp., chopped
- Fresh parsley - ¼ cup, chopped
- Dry milk – 3 tbsp.
- Sugar – 2 tbsp.
- Salt – 1 tsp.
- Bread machine yeast – 1 ½ tsp.

Directions:
1. Add everything according to bread machine recommendations.
2. Select Basic/White cycle and Medium or Light crust.
3. Remove the bread when done.
4. Cool, slice, and serve.

Nutrition Info: (Per Serving): Calories: 100; Total Fat: 2 g; Saturated Fat: 1 g; Carbohydrates: 21 g; Cholesterol: 5 mg; Fiber: 3 g; Calcium: 75 mg; Sodium: 220 mg; Protein: 1 g

Caramelized Onion Bread

Servings: 14 Slices
Cooking Time: 3 H. 35 Min.
Ingredients:

- ½ Tbsp butter
- ½ cup onions, sliced
- 1 cup water
- 1 Tbsp olive oil
- 3 cups Gold Medal Better for Bread flour
- 2 Tbsp sugar
- 1 tsp salt
- 1¼ tsp bread machine or quick active dry yeast

Directions:
1. Melt the butter over medium-low heat in a skillet.
2. Cook the onions in the butter for 10 to 15 minutes until they are brown and caramelized - then remove from the heat.
3. Add each ingredient except the onions to the bread machine in the order and at the temperature recommended by your bread machine manufacturer.
4. Close the lid, select the basic bread, medium crust setting on your bread machine and press start.
5. Add ½ cup of onions 5 to 10 minutes before the last kneading cycle ends.
6. When the bread machine has finished baking, remove the bread and put it on a cooling rack.

Caraway Rye Bread

Servings: 1 Loaf
Cooking Time: 10 Minutes
Ingredients:
- 12 slice bread (1½ pounds)
- 1⅛ cups water, at 80°F to 90°F
- 1¾ tablespoons melted butter, cooled
- 3 tablespoons dark brown sugar
- 1½ tablespoons dark molasses
- 1⅛ teaspoons salt
- 1½ teaspoons caraway seed
- ¾ cup dark rye flour
- 2 cups white bread flour
- 1⅛ teaspoons bread machine or instant yeast

Directions:
1. Preparing the Ingredients.
2. Choose the size of loaf of your preference and then measure the ingredients.
3. Add all of the ingredients mentioned previously in the list.
4. Close the lid after placing the pan in the bread machine.
5. Select the Bake cycle
6. Turn on the bread machine. Select the White/Basic setting, select the loaf size, and the crust color. Press start.
7. When the cycle is finished, carefully remove the pan from the bread maker and let it rest.
8. Remove the bread from the pan, put in a wire rack to Cool about 10 minutes. Slice

CHEESE & SWEET BREAD

Chocolate Cherry Bread

Servings: 14 Slices
Cooking Time: 30 Minutes Plus Fermenting Time
Ingredients:
- 1 cup milk
- 1 egg
- 3 Tbsp water
- 4 tsp butter
- ½ tsp almond extract
- 4 cups bread flour
- 3 Tbsp sugar
- 1 tsp salt
- 1¼ tsp active dry yeast
- ½ cup dried cherries, snipped
- ½ cup semisweet chocolate pieces, chilled

Directions:
1. Preparing the Ingredients
2. Add each ingredient to the bread machine in the order and at the temperature recommended by your
3. bread machine manufacturer.
4. Select the Bake cycle
5. Close the lid, select the sweet loaf, low crust setting on your bread machine, and press start.
6. When the bread machine has finished baking, remove the bread and put it on a cooling rack.

Candied Fruits Bread

Servings: 12
Cooking Time: 3 Hours And 25 Minutes
Ingredients:
- Orange juice - 1 cup
- Lukewarm water - ½ cup
- Butter - 2½ tbsp., softened
- Powdered milk - 2 tbsp.
- Brown sugar - 2½ tbsp.
- Kosher salt - 1 tsp.
- Whole-grain flour - 4 cups
- Bread machine yeast - 1½ tsp.
- Candied fruits - ¾ cup (pineapple, coconut, papaya)
- Walnuts - ¼ cup, chopped
- All-purpose flour - 1 tbsp. for packing candied fruits
- Almond flakes - ¼ cup

Directions:
1. Put the candied fruit water, then dry on a paper towel and roll in flour.
2. Add everything in the bread machine pan (except almonds and fruit) according to bread machine recommendations.

3. Select Basic and Medium crust.
4. Add the almonds and fruit after the beep.
5. Remove the bread when done.
6. Cool, slice, and serve.

Nutrition Info: (Per Serving): Calories: 313; Total Fat: 4.3 g; Saturated Fat: 2.4 g;Carbohydrates: 60.2 g; Cholesterol: 10 mg; Fiber: 1.9 g; Calcium: 42 mg; Sodium: 331 mg; Protein: 7.8 g

Mexican Chocolate Bread

Servings: 1 Loaf
Cooking Time: 10 Minutes Plus Fermenting Time
Ingredients:
- ½ cup milk
- ½ cup orange juice
- 1 large egg plus 1 egg yolk
- 3 Tbsp unsalted butter cut into pieces
- 2½ cups bread flour
- ¼ cup light brown sugar
- 3 Tbsp unsweetened dutch-process cocoa powder
- 1 Tbsp gluten
- 1 tsp instant espresso powder
- ¾ tsp ground cinnamon
- ½ cup bittersweet chocolate chips
- 2½ tsp bread machine yeast

Directions:
1. Preparing the Ingredients.
2. Add each ingredient to the bread machine in the order and at the temperature recommended by your bread machine manufacturer.
3. Select the Bake cycle
4. Close the lid, select the sweet loaf, low crust setting on your bread machine, and press start.
5. When the bread machine has finished baking, remove the bread and put it on a cooling rack.

Coconut Ginger Bread

Servings: 1 Loaf
Cooking Time: 1 Hour
Ingredients:
- 1 cup + 2 tbsp Half & Half
- One ¼ cup toasted shredded coconut
- Two large eggs
- ¼ cup oil
- 1 tsp coconut extract
- 1 tsp lemon extract
- 3/4 cup sugar
- 1 tbsp grated lemon peel
- 2 cups all-purpose flour
- 2 tbsp finely chopped candied ginger

- 1 tbsp baking powder
- ½ tsp salt
- One ¼ cup toasted shredded coconut

Directions:
1. Put everything in your bread machine pan.
2. Select the quick bread mode.
3. Press the start button.
4. Allow bread to cool on the wire rack until ready to serve (at least 20 minutes).

Nutrition Info: Calories 210;Carbohydrates: 45g;Total Fat 3g;Cholesterol3mg;Protein 5g;Fiber 2g;Sugar 15g;Sodium 185mg;Potassium 61mg

Chocolate Sour Cream Bread

Servings: 1 Loaf
Cooking Time: 20 Minutes Plus Fermenting Time
Ingredients:
- 12 slice bread (1½ pounds)
- 1 cup sour cream
- 2 eggs, at room temperature
- 1 cup sugar
- ½ cup (1 stick) butter, at room temperature
- ¼ cup plain Greek yogurt
- 1¾ cups all-purpose flour
- ½ cup unsweetened cocoa powder
- ½ teaspoon baking powder
- ½ teaspoon salt
- 1 cup milk chocolate chips

Directions:
1. Preparing the Ingredients.
2. In a small bowl, whisk together the sour cream, eggs, sugar, butter, and yogurt until just combined.
3. Transfer the wet ingredients to the bread machine bucket, and then add the flour, cocoa powder, baking powder, salt, and chocolate chips. Program the machine for Quick/Rapid bread, and press Start. When the loaf is done, stick a knife into it, and if it comes out clean, the loaf is done.
4. Select the Bake cycle
5. If the loaf needs a few more minutes, check the control panel for a Bake Only button and extend the time by 10 minutes.
6. When the loaf is done, remove the bucket from the machine. Let the loaf cool for 5 minutes. Gently shake the bucket to remove the loaf, and turn it out onto a rack to cool.

Easy Donuts

Servings: 12
Cooking Time: 1 Hour
Ingredients:
- 2/3 cups milk, room temperature

44

- 1/4 cup water, room temperature
- ½ cup of warm water
- 1/4 cup softened butter
- One egg slightly has beaten
- 1/4 cup granulated sugar
- 1 tsp salt
- 3 cups bread machine flour
- 2 1/2 tsp bread machine yeast
- oil for deep frying
- 1/4 cup confectioners' sugar

Directions:
1. Place the milk, water, butter, egg sugar, salt, flour, and yeast in a pan.
2. Select dough setting and push start. Press the start button.
3. When the process is complete, remove dough from the pan and transfer it to a lightly floured surface.
4. Using a rolling pin lightly dusted with flour, roll dough to ½ inch thickness.
5. Cut with a floured dusted donut cutter or circle cookie cutter.
6. Transfer donuts to a baking sheet that has been covered with wax paper. Place another layer of paper on top, then cover with a clean tea towel. Let rise 30-40 minutes.
7. Heat vegetable oil to 375º (190ºCº) in a deep-fryer or large, heavy pot.
8. Fry donuts 2-3 at a time until golden brown on both sides for about 3 minutes.
9. Drain on a paper towel.
10. Sprinkle with confectioners' sugar.

Nutrition Info: Calories 180;Carbohydrates: 30g;Total Fat 5g;Cholesterol 25mg;Protein 4g;Fiber 2g;Sugar 7g;Sodium 240mg;Potassium 64mg

Cheese Jalapeno Bread

Servings: 10
Cooking Time: 2 Hours
Ingredients:
- Monterey jack cheese – ¼ cup, shredded
- Active dry yeast – 2 tsps.
- Butter – 1 ½ tbsps.
- Sugar – 1 ½ tbsps.
- Milk – 3 tbsps.
- Flour – 3 cups.
- Water – 1 cup.
- Jalapeno pepper – 1, minced
- Salt – 1 ½ tsps.

Directions:
1. Add all ingredients to the bread machine pan according to the bread machine manufacturer instructions. Select basic bread setting then select light/medium crust and start. Once loaf is done, remove the loaf pan from the machine. Allow it to cool for 10 minutes. Slice and serve.

Cheddar Cheese Bread

Servings: 20
Cooking Time: 3 Hours And 25 Minutes
Ingredients:
- Water – ¾ cup
- Egg – 1
- Salt – 1 tsp.
- Bread flour – 3 cups
- Shredded sharp cheddar cheese – 1 cup
- Nonfat dry milk – 2 tbsp.
- Sugar – 2 tbsp.
- Bread machine yeast – 1 tsp.

Directions:
1. Add everything according to bread machine recommendations.
2. Select Basic/White bread and Medium crust.
3. Remove the bread when done.
4. Cool, slice, and serve.

Nutrition Info: (Per Serving): Calories: 101; Total Fat: 2.3 g; Saturated Fat: 1.3 g; Carbohydrates: 15.8 g; Cholesterol: 15 mg; Fiber: 0.6 g; Calcium: 48 mg; Sodium: 157 mg; Protein: 3.8 g

Cheddar Cheese Basil Bread

Servings: 1 Loaf
Cooking Time: 10 Minutes
Ingredients:
- 12 slice bread (1½ pounds)
- 1 cup milk, at 80°F to 90°F
- 1 tablespoon melted butter, cooled
- 1 tablespoon sugar
- 1 teaspoon dried basil
- ¾ cup (3 ounces) shredded sharp Cheddar cheese
- ¾ teaspoon salt
- 3 cups white bread flour
- 1½ teaspoons bread machine or active dry yeast

Directions:
1. Preparing the Ingredients.
2. Choose the size of loaf of your preference and then measure the ingredients.
3. Add all of the ingredients mentioned previously in the list.
4. Close the lid after placing the pan in the bread machine.
5. Select the Bake cycle
6. Turn on the bread machine. Select the White/Basic setting, select the loaf size, and the crust color. Press start.
7. When the cycle is finished, carefully remove the pan from the bread maker and let it rest.
8. Remove the bread from the pan, put in a wire rack to Cool about 5 minutes. Slice

Vanilla Almond Milk Bread

Servings: 1 Loaf
Cooking Time: 10 Minutes Plus Fermenting Time
Ingredients:
- 12 slice bread (1½ pounds)
- ½ cup plus 1 tablespoon milk, at 80°F to 90°F
- 3 tablespoons melted butter, cooled
- 3 tablespoons sugar
- 1 egg, at room temperature
- 1½ teaspoons pure vanilla extract
- ⅓ teaspoon almond extract
- 2½ cups white bread flour
- 1½ teaspoons bread machine or instant yeast

Directions:
1. Preparing the Ingredients.
2. Choose the size of loaf of your preference and then measure the ingredients.
3. Add all of the ingredients mentioned previously in the list.
4. Close the lid after placing the pan in the bread machine.
5. Select the Bake cycle
6. Turn on the bread machine. Select the Sweet setting, select the loaf size, and the crust color. Press start.
7. When the cycle is finished, carefully remove the pan from the bread maker and let it rest.
8. Remove the bread from the pan, put in a wire rack to Cool about 5 minutes. Slice

Crusty Mustard Focaccia

Servings: 8 Slices
Cooking Time: 10 Minutes Plus Fermenting Time
Ingredients:
- 2/3 cup water
- 1 tablespoon olive or vegetable oil
- 2 tablespoons spicy mustard
- 2¼ cups bread flour
- 1 tablespoon sugar
- 1 teaspoon table salt
- 1½ teaspoons bread machine or fast-acting dry yeast
- 3 tablespoons olive or vegetable oil
- Coarse (kosher or sea) salt, if desired

Directions:
1. Preparing the Ingredients.
2. Measure carefully, placing all ingredients except 3 tablespoons oil and the coarse salt in bread machine pan in the order recommended by the manufacturer.
3. Select Dough/Manual cycle. Do not use delay cycle.
4. Remove dough from pan, using lightly floured hands. Knead 5 minutes on lightly floured surface (if necessary, knead in enough additional flour to make dough easy to handle). Cover and let rest 10 minutes.
5. Select the Bake cycle

6. Grease large cookie sheet. Roll or pat dough into 12-inch round on cookie sheet. Cover and let rise in warm place 10 minutes or until almost double.
7. Heat oven to 400°F. Prick dough with fork at 1-inch intervals or make deep depressions in dough with fingertips. Brush with 3 tablespoons oil. Sprinkle with coarse salt. Bake 15 to 18 minutes or until golden brown. Serve warm or cool.

Ricotta Bread

Servings: 14 Slices
Cooking Time: 3 H. 15 Min.
Ingredients:
- 3 Tbsp skim milk
- ⅔ cup ricotta cheese
- 4 tsp unsalted butter, softened to room temperature
- 1 large egg
- 2 Tbsp granulated sugar
- ½ tsp salt
- 1½ cups bread flour, + more flour, as needed
- 1 tsp active dry yeast

Directions:
1. Add each ingredient to the bread machine in the order and at the temperature recommended by your bread machine manufacturer.
2. Close the lid, select the basic bread, medium crust setting on your bread machine, and press start.
3. When the bread machine has finished baking, remove the bread and put it on a cooling rack.

Jalapeno Cheese Bread

Servings: 14 Slices
Cooking Time: 3 H.
Ingredients:
- 3 cups bread flour
- 1½ tsp active dry yeast
- 1 cup water
- 2 Tbsp sugar
- 1 tsp salt
- ½ cup shredded cheddar cheese
- ¼ cup diced jalapeno peppers

Directions:
1. Add each ingredient to the bread machine in the order and at the temperature recommended by your bread machine manufacturer.
2. Close the lid, select the basic bread, medium crust setting on your bread machine, and press start.
3. When the bread machine has finished baking, remove the bread and put it on a cooling rack.

Roasted Garlic Asiago Bread

Servings: 1 Loaf
Cooking Time: 10 Minutes
Ingredients:
- 12 slice bread (1½ pounds)
- ¾ cup plus 1 tablespoon milk, at 70°F to 80°F
- ¼ cup melted butter, cooled
- 1 teaspoon minced garlic
- 2 tablespoons sugar
- 1 teaspoon salt
- ½ cup (2 ounces) grated Asiago cheese
- 2¾ cups white bread flour
- 1½ teaspoons bread machine or instant yeast
- ½ cup mashed roasted garlic

Directions:
1. Preparing the Ingredients.
2. Choose the size of loaf of your preference and then measure the ingredients.
3. Add all of the ingredients mentioned previously in the list.
4. Close the lid after placing the pan in the bread machine.
5. Select the Bake cycle
6. Turn on the bread machine. Select the White/Basic setting, select the loaf size, and the crust color. Press start.
7. When the cycle is finished, carefully remove the pan from the bread maker and let it rest.
8. Remove the bread from the pan, put in a wire rack to Cool about 5 minutes. Slice

Moist Cheddar Cheese Bread

Servings: 10
Cooking Time: 3 Hours 45 Minutes
Ingredients:
- Milk – 1 cup
- Butter – ½ cup, melted
- All-purpose flour – 3 cups
- Cheddar cheese – 2 cups, shredded
- Garlic powder – ½ tsp.
- Kosher salt – 2 tsps.
- Sugar – 1 tbsp.
- Active dry yeast – 1 ¼ oz.

Directions:
1. Add milk and butter into the bread pan. Add remaining ingredients except for yeast to the bread pan. Make a small hole into the flour with your finger and add yeast to the hole. Make sure yeast will not be mixed with any liquids. Select basic setting then select light crust and start. Once loaf is done, remove the loaf pan from the machine. Allow it to cool for 10 minutes. Slice and serve.

Feta Oregano Bread

Servings: 1 Loaf
Cooking Time: 10 Minutes Plus Fermenting Time
Ingredients:
- 8 slice bread (1 pounds)
- ⅔ cup milk, at 80°F to 90°F
- 2 teaspoons melted butter, cooled
- 2 teaspoons sugar
- ⅔ teaspoon salt
- 2 teaspoons dried oregano
- 2 cups white bread flour
- 1½ teaspoons bread machine or instant yeast
- ⅔ cup (2½ ounces) crumbled feta cheese

Directions:
1. Preparing the Ingredients.
2. Choose the size of loaf of your preference and then measure the ingredients.
3. Add all of the ingredients mentioned previously in the list.
4. Close the lid after placing the pan in the bread machine.
5. Select the Bake cycle
6. Turn on the bread machine. Select the Quick/Rapid setting, select the loaf size, and the crust color. Press start.
7. When the cycle is finished, carefully remove the pan from the bread maker and let it rest.
8. Remove the bread from the pan, put in a wire rack to Cool about 5 minutes. Slice

American Cheese Beer Bread

Servings: 1 Loaf
Ingredients:
- 16 slice bread (2 pounds)
- 1⅔ cups warm beer
- 1½ tablespoons sugar
- 2 teaspoons table salt
- 1½ tablespoons unsalted butter, melted
- ¾ cup American cheese, shredded
- ¾ cup Monterrey Jack cheese, shredded
- 4 cups white bread flour
- 2 teaspoons bread machine yeast
- 12 slice bread (1½ pounds)
- 1¼ cups warm beer
- 1 tablespoon sugar
- 1½ teaspoons table salt
- 1 tablespoon unsalted butter, melted
- ½ cup American cheese, shredded
- ½ cup Monterrey Jack cheese, shredded
- 3 cups white bread flour
- 1½ teaspoons bread machine yeast

Directions:

1. Choose the size of loaf you would like to make and measure your ingredients.
2. Add the ingredients to the bread pan in the order listed above.
3. Place the pan in the bread machine and close the lid.
4. Turn on the bread maker. Select the White/Basic setting, then the loaf size, and finally the crust color. Start the cycle.
5. When the cycle is finished and the bread is baked, carefully remove the pan from the machine. Use a potholder as the handle will be very hot. Let rest for a few minutes.
6. Remove the bread from the pan and allow to cool on a wire rack for at least 10 minutes before slicing.

Nutrition Info: (Per Serving):Calories 173, fat 5.3 g, carbs 26.1 g, sodium 118 mg, protein 6.2 g

Cheesy Chipotle Bread

Servings: 1 Loaf
Cooking Time: 10 Minutes
Ingredients:
- 8 slice bread (1 pounds)
- ⅔ cup water, at 80°F to 90°F
- 1½ tablespoons sugar
- 1½ tablespoons powdered skim milk
- ¾ teaspoon salt
- ½ teaspoon chipotle chili powder
- 2 cups white bread flour
- ½ cup (2 ounces) shredded sharp Cheddar cheese
- ¾ teaspoon bread machine or instant yeast

Directions:
1. Preparing the Ingredients.
2. Choose the size of loaf of your preference and then measure the ingredients.
3. Add all of the ingredients mentioned previously in the list.
4. Close the lid after placing the pan in the bread machine.
5. Select the Bake cycle
6. Turn on the bread machine. Select the White/Basic setting, select the loaf size, and the crust color. Press start.
7. When the cycle is finished, carefully remove the pan from the bread maker and let it rest.
8. Remove the bread from the pan, put in a wire rack to Cool about 5 minutes. Slice

Choco Chip Bread

Servings: 10
Cooking Time: 2 Hours
Ingredients:
- Yeast – 1 ½ tsps.
- Bread flour – 3 cups.
- Brown sugar – 2 tbsps.
- Sugar – 2 tbsps.
- Salt – 1 tsp.
- Ground cinnamon – 1 tsp.

- Butter – 4 tbsps., softened
- Egg – 1, slightly beaten
- Warm milk – 1 cup.
- Water – ¼ cup.
- Chocolate chips – 1 cup.

Directions:
1. Add all ingredients except for chocolate chips into the bread machine pan. Select basic setting then select light crust and press start. Add chocolate chips just before the final kneading cycle. Once loaf is done, remove the loaf pan from the machine. Allow it to cool for 10 minutes. Slice and serve.

Oregano Cheese Bread

Servings: 1 Loaf
Cooking Time: 10 Minutes
Ingredients:
- 3 cups bread flour
- 1 cup water
- ½ cup freshly grated parmesan cheese
- 3 Tbsp sugar
- 1 Tbsp dried leaf oregano
- 1½ Tbsp olive oil
- 1 tsp salt
- 2 tsp active dry yeast

Directions:
1. Preparing the Ingredients
2. Add each ingredient to the bread machine in the order and at the temperature recommended by your bread machine manufacturer.
3. Select the Bake cycle
4. Close the lid, select the basic bread, medium crust setting on your bread machine, and press start.
5. When the bread machine has finished baking, remove the bread and put it on a cooling rack.

Sweet Banana Bread

Servings: 10
Cooking Time: 2 Hours
Ingredients:
- Warm milk – ½ cup.
- Vanilla extract – 1 tsp.
- Butter – 8 tbsps.
- Eggs – 2
- Salt – ½ tsp.
- All-purpose flour – 2 cups.
- Sugar – 1 cup.
- Bananas – 3, mashed
- Baking soda – 1 tsp.

- Baking powder – 2 tsps.

Directions:
1. Add all ingredients into the bread machine pan. Select quick bread setting then select light crust and press start. Once loaf is done, remove the loaf pan from the machine. Allow it to cool for 10 minutes. Slice and serve.

Simple Cottage Cheese Bread

Servings: 1 Loaf
Cooking Time: 10 Minutes Plus Fermenting Time
Ingredients:
- 12 slice bread (1½ pounds)
- ½ cup water, at 80°F to 90°F
- ¾ cup cottage cheese, at room temperature
- 1 egg, at room temperature
- 2 tablespoons butter, melted and cooled
- 1 tablespoon sugar
- 1 teaspoon salt
- ¼ teaspoon baking soda
- 3 cups white bread flour
- 2 teaspoons bread machine or instant yeast

Directions:
1. Preparing the Ingredients.
2. Choose the size of loaf of your preference and then measure the ingredients.
3. Add all of the ingredients mentioned previously in the list.
4. Close the lid after placing the pan in the bread machine.
5. Select the Bake cycle
6. Turn on the bread machine. Select the White/Basic setting, select the loaf size, and the crust color. Press start.
7. When the cycle is finished, carefully remove the pan from the bread maker and let it rest.
8. Remove the bread from the pan, put in a wire rack to Cool about 5 minutes. Slice

Gluten-free Cheesy Bread

Servings: 10
Cooking Time: 4 Hours
Ingredients:
- Eggs – 3
- Olive oil – 2 tbsps.
- Water – 1 ½ cups.
- Active dry yeast – 2 ¼ tsp.
- White rice flour – 2 cups.
- Brown rice flour – 1 cup.
- Milk powder – ¼ cup.
- Sugar – 2 tbsps.
- Poppy seeds – 1 tbsp.
- Xanthan gum – 3 ½ tsps.
- Cheddar cheese – 1 ½ cups., shredded
- Salt – 1 tsp.

Directions:

1. In a medium bowl, mix together eggs, water, and oil and pour it into the bread machine pan. In a large bowl, mix together remaining ingredients and pour over wet ingredient mixture into the bread pan. Select whole wheat setting then select light/medium crust and start. Once loaf is done, remove the loaf pan from the machine. Allow it to cool for 10 minutes. Slice and serve.

Honey Goat Cheese Bread

Servings: 1 Loaf
Cooking Time: 10 Minutes Plus Fermenting Time
Ingredients:
*   12 slice bread (1½ pounds)
*   1 cup lukewarm milk
*   1½ tablespoons honey
*   1 teaspoon table salt
*   1 teaspoon freshly cracked black pepper
*   ¼ cup goat cheese, shredded or crumbled
*   3 cups white bread flour
*   1½ teaspoons bread machine yeast

Directions:
1. Preparing the Ingredients.
2. Choose the size of loaf of your preference and then measure the ingredients.
3. Add all of the ingredients mentioned previously in the list.
4. Close the lid after placing the pan in the bread machine.
5. Select the Bake cycle
6. Turn on the bread machine. Select the Quick/Rapid setting, select the loaf size, and the crust color. Press start.
7. When the cycle is finished, carefully remove the pan from the bread maker and let it rest.
8. Remove the bread from the pan, put in a wire rack to Cool about 5 minutes. Slice

Basil Cheese Bread

Servings: 1 Loaf
Cooking Time: 10 Minutes Plus Fermenting Time
Ingredients:
*   12 slice bread (1½ pounds)
*   1 cup lukewarm milk
*   1 tablespoon unsalted butter, melted
*   1 tablespoon sugar
*   1 teaspoon dried basil
*   ¾ teaspoon table salt
*   ¾ cup sharp Cheddar cheese, shredded
*   3 cups white bread flour
*   1½ teaspoons bread machine yeast

Directions:
1. Preparing the Ingredients.
2. Choose the size of loaf of your preference and then measure the ingredients.
3. Add all of the ingredients mentioned previously in the list.
4. Close the lid after placing the pan in the bread machine.
5. Select the Bake cycle

6. Turn on the bread machine. Select the Quick/Rapid setting, select the loaf size, and the crust color. Press start.
7. When the cycle is finished, carefully remove the pan from the bread maker and let it rest.
8. Remove the bread from the pan, put in a wire rack to Cool about 5 minutes. Slice

Mexican Style Jalapeno Cheese Bread

Servings: 1 Loaf
Ingredients:
- 16 slice bread (2 pounds)
- 1 small jalapeno pepper, seeded and minced
- 1 cup lukewarm water
- 3 tablespoons nonfat dry milk powder
- 1½ tablespoons unsalted butter, melted
- 1½ tablespoons sugar
- 1½ teaspoons table salt
- ¼ cup finely shredded cheese (Mexican blend or Monterrey Jack)
- 3 cups white bread flour
- 2 teaspoons bread machine yeast
- 12 slice bread (1½ pounds)
- 1 small jalapeno pepper, seeded and minced
- ¾ cup lukewarm water
- 2 tablespoons nonfat dry milk powder
- 1 tablespoon unsalted butter, melted
- 1 tablespoon sugar
- 1 teaspoon salt
- 3 tablespoons finely shredded cheese (Mexican blend or Monterrey Jack)
- 2 cups white bread flour
- 1½ teaspoons bread machine yeast

Directions:
1. Choose the size of loaf you would like to make and measure your ingredients.
2. Add the ingredients to the bread pan in the order listed above.
3. Place the pan in the bread machine and close the lid.
4. Turn on the bread maker. Select the White/Basic setting, then the loaf size, and finally the crust color. Start the cycle.
5. When the cycle is finished and the bread is baked, carefully remove the pan from the machine. Use a potholder as the handle will be very hot. Let rest for a few minutes.
6. Remove the bread from the pan and allow to cool on a wire rack for at least 10 minutes before slicing.
Nutrition Info: (Per Serving):Calories 220, fat 9.4 g, carbs 18.6 g, sodium 206 mg, protein 9 g

Rich Cheddar Bread

Servings: 1 Loaf
Cooking Time: 10 Minutes Plus Fermenting Time
Ingredients:
- 12 slice bread (1½ pounds)
- 1 cup milk, at 80°F to 90°F
- 2 tablespoons butter, melted and cooled
- 3 tablespoons sugar

- 1 teaspoon salt
- ½ cup (2 ounces) grated aged Cheddar cheese
- 3 cups white bread flour
- 2 teaspoons bread machine or instant yeast

Directions:
1. Preparing the Ingredients.
2. Choose the size of loaf of your preference and then measure the ingredients.
3. Add all of the ingredients mentioned previously in the list.
4. Close the lid after placing the pan in the bread machine.
5. Select the Bake cycle
6. Turn on the bread machine. Select the Quick/Rapid setting, select the loaf size, and the crust color. Press start.
7. When the cycle is finished, carefully remove the pan from the bread maker and let it rest.
8. Remove the bread from the pan, put in a wire rack to Cool about 5 minutes. Slice

Beer And Pretzel Bread

Servings: 12 Slices
Cooking Time: 10 Minutes Plus Fermenting Time
Ingredients:
- ¾ cup regular or nonalcoholic beer
- 1/3 cup water
- 2 tablespoons butter, softened
- 3 cups bread flour
- 1 tablespoon packed brown sugar
- 1 teaspoon ground mustard
- 1 teaspoon salt
- 1½ teaspoons bread machine yeast
- ½ cup bite-size pretzel pieces, about 1×¾ inch, or pretzel rods, cut into 1-inch pieces

Directions:
1. Preparing the Ingredients.
2. Measure carefully, placing all ingredients except pretzels in bread machine pan in order recommended by the manufacturer.
3. Select the Bake cycle
4. Select Basic/White cycle. Use Medium or Light crust color. Do not use delay cycle.
5. Add pretzels 5 minutes before the last kneading cycle ends. Remove baked bread from pan; cool on cooling rack.

Peach Bread

Servings: 10
Cooking Time: 3 Hours And 48 Minutes
Ingredients:
- Wholemeal flour – 4 cups
- Bread machine yeast – 2 tsp.
- Lukewarm water – 1 ¼ cups
- Flaxseed oil – 1 ½ tsp.
- Brown sugar – 1 ½ tsp.
- Kosher salt – 1 ½ tsp.
- Peaches – 2, peeled and diced

Directions:
1. Add everything in the bread machine (except the peaches) according to bread machine recommendations.
2. Select Whole-Grain and Medium crust.
3. Add the peaches after the beep.
4. Remove the bread when done.
5. Cool, slice, and serve.

Nutrition Info: (Per Serving): Calories: 246; Total Fat: 4 g; Saturated Fat: 0.3 g; Carbohydrates: 44.3 g; Cholesterol: 0 mg; Fiber: 6.4 g; Calcium: 50 mg; Sodium: 440 mg; Protein: 8.2 g

Apple Honey Bread

Servings: 1 Loaf
Cooking Time: 10 Minutes Plus Fermenting Time

Ingredients:
*   12 slice bread (1½ pounds)
*   5 tablespoons lukewarm milk
*   3 tablespoons apple cider, at room temperature
*   3 tablespoons sugar
*   2 tablespoons unsalted butter, melted
*   1½ tablespoons honey
*   ¼ teaspoon table salt
*   3 cups white bread flour
*   1¼ teaspoons bread machine yeast
*   1 apple, peeled, cored, and finely diced

Directions:
1. Preparing the Ingredients.
2. Choose the size of loaf of your preference and then measure the ingredients.
3. Add all of the ingredients mentioned previously in the list, except for the apples. Close the lid after placing the pan in the bread machine.
4. Select the Bake cycle
5. Turn on the bread maker. Select the White/Basic or Fruit/Nut (if your machine has this setting) setting, then the loaf size, and finally the crust color. Start the cycle.
6. When the machine signals to add ingredients, add the apples. When the cycle is finished, carefully remove the pan from the bread maker and let it rest. Remove the bread from the pan, put in a wire rack to Cool about 5 minutes. Slice

GLUTEN-FREE BREAD

Cinnamon Raisin Bread

Servings: 1 Loaf (12 Slices)
Cooking Time: 1 Hour
Ingredients:
- 300ml (1 ¼ cups) warm water
- 60ml (¼ cup) olive oil
- Two tablespoons honey
- Two egg whites
- One tablespoon apple cider vinegar
- ½ teaspoon baking powder
- 7g (2 teaspoons) dry active yeast
- Two tablespoons granulated sugar
- 200g (2 cups) gluten-free almond flour / or any other gluten-free flour, levelled
- 100g (1 cup) Tapioca/potato starch, levelled
- Two teaspoons Xanthan Gum
- One teaspoon salt
- One teaspoon ground cinnamon
- 150g (1 cup) raisins

Directions:
1. According to your bread machine manufacturer, place all the ingredients into the bread machine's greased pan except raisins.
2. Select basic cycle / standard cycle/bake / quick bread / sweet bread setting
3. then choose crust colour either medium or Light and press start to bake bread.
4. In the last kneading cycle, check the dough
5. it should be wet but thick, not like traditional bread dough. If the dough is too wet, put more flour, one tablespoon at a time, or until dough slightly firm.
6. Add raisins 5 minutes before the kneading cycle ends.
7. When the cycle is finished and the machine turns off, remove baked bread from pan and cool on wire rack.

Nutrition Info: Calories: 89 Calories;Fat: 1 g;Cholesterol: 2 mg;Sodium: 10 mg;Carbohydrates: 12 g

Gluten-free Potato Bread

Servings: 12
Cooking Time: 3 Hours
Ingredients:
- 1 medium russet potato, baked, or mashed leftovers
- 2 packets gluten-free quick yeast
- 3 tablespoons honey
- 3/4 cup warm almond milk
- 2 eggs, 1 egg white
- 3 2/3 cups almond flour
- 3/4 cup tapioca flour
- 1 teaspoon sea salt

- 1 teaspoon dried chives
- 1 tablespoon apple cider vinegar
- 1/4 cup olive oil

Directions:
1. Combine all of the dry ingredients, except the yeast, in a large mixing bowl; set aside.
2. Whisk together the milk, eggs, oil, apple cider, and honey in a separate mixing bowl.
3. Pour the wet ingredients into the bread maker.
4. Add the dry ingredients on top of the wet ingredients.
5. Create a well in the dry ingredients and add the yeast.
6. Set to Gluten-Free bread setting, light crust color, and press Start.
7. Allow to cool completely before slicing.

Nutrition Info: Calories: 232, Sodium: 173 mg, Dietary Fiber: 6.3 g, Fat: 13.2 g, Carbs: 17.4 g, Protein: 10.4 g.

Gluten-free Sourdough Bread

Servings: 12
Cooking Time: 3 Hours
Ingredients:
- 1 cup water
- 3 eggs
- 3/4 cup ricotta cheese
- 1/4 cup honey
- 1/4 cup vegetable oil
- 1 teaspoon cider vinegar
- 3/4 cup gluten-free sourdough starter
- 2 cups white rice flour
- 2/3 cup potato starch
- 1/3 cup tapioca flour
- 1/2 cup dry milk powder
- 3 1/2 teaspoons xanthan gum
- 1 1/2 teaspoons salt

Directions:
1. Combine wet ingredients and pour into bread maker pan.
2. Mix together dry ingredients in a large mixing bowl, and add on top of the wet ingredients.
3. Select Gluten-Free cycle and press Start.
4. Remove the pan from the machine and allow the bread to remain in the pan for approximately 10 minutes.
5. Transfer to a cooling rack before slicing.

Nutrition Info: Calories: 299, Sodium: 327 mg, Dietary Fiber: 1.0 g, Fat: 7.3 g, Carbs: 46 g, Protein: 5.2 g.

Gluten-free Cinnamon Raisin Bread

Servings: 12
Cooking Time: 3 Hours
Ingredients:

- 3/4 cup almond milk
- 2 tablespoons flax meal
- 6 tablespoons warm water
- 1 1/2 teaspoons apple cider vinegar
- 2 tablespoons butter
- 1 1/2 tablespoons honey
- 1 2/3 cups brown rice flour
- 1/4 cup corn starch
- 2 tablespoons potato starch
- 1 1/2 teaspoons xanthan gum
- 1 tablespoon cinnamon
- 1/2 teaspoon salt
- 1 teaspoon active dry yeast
- 1/2 cup raisins

Directions:
1. Mix together flax and water and let stand for 5 minutes.
2. Combine dry ingredients in a separate bowl, except for yeast.
3. Add wet ingredients to the bread machine.
4. Add the dry mixture on top and make a well in the middle of the dry mixture.
5. Add the yeast to the well.
6. Set to Gluten Free, light crust color, and press Start.
7. After first kneading and rise cycle, add raisins.
8. Remove to a cooling rack when baked and let cool for 15 minutes before slicing.

Nutrition Info: Calories: 192, Sodium: 173 mg, Dietary Fiber: 4.4 g, Fat: 4.7 g, Carbs: 38.2 g, Protein: 2.7 g.

Sandwich Bread

Servings: 1 Loaf (16 Slices).
Cooking Time: 1 Hour
Ingredients:
- 1 tbsp. active dry yeast
- 2 tbsps. sugar
- 1 cup warm fat-free milk (110° to 115°)
- Two eggs
- 3 tbsps. canola oil
- 1 tsp. cider vinegar
- 2-1/2 cups gluten-free all-purpose baking flour
- 2-1/2 tsp. xanthan gum
- 1 tsp. unflavored gelatin
- 1/2 tsp. salt

Directions:
1. Oil a loaf pan, 9x5 inches in size, and dust with gluten-free flour reserve.
2. In warm milk, melt sugar and yeast in a small bowl—mix yeast mixture, vinegar, oil, and eggs in a stand with a paddle. Slowly whip in salt, gelatin, xanthan gum and flour. Whip for a minute on low speed. Whip for 2 minutes on moderate. The dough will become softer compared to the yeast bread dough that has gluten. Turn onto the prepped pan. Using a wet spatula,

smoothen the surface. Put a cover and rise in a warm area for 25 minutes until dough extends to the pan top.

3. Bake for 20 minutes at 375°
4. loosely cover with foil. Bake till golden brown for 10 to 15 minutes more. Take out from pan onto a wire rack to let cool.

Nutrition Info: Calories: 110 calories;Total Carbohydrate: 17 g;Cholesterol: 27 mg;Total Fat: 4 g;Fiber: 2 g;Protein: 4 g;Sodium: 95 mg

Gluten-free Whole Grain Bread

Servings: 12
Cooking Time: 3 Hours 40 Minutes
Ingredients:
- 2/3 cup sorghum flour
- 1/2 cup buckwheat flour
- 1/2 cup millet flour
- 3/4 cup potato starch
- 2 1/4 teaspoons xanthan gum
- 1 1/4 teaspoons salt
- 3/4 cup skim milk
- 1/2 cup water
- 1 tablespoon instant yeast
- 5 teaspoons agave nectar, separated
- 1 large egg, lightly beaten
- 4 tablespoons extra virgin olive oil
- 1/2 teaspoon cider vinegar
- 1 tablespoon poppy seeds

Directions:
1. Whisk sorghum, buckwheat, millet, potato starch, xanthan gum, and sea salt in a bowl and set aside.
2. Combine milk and water in a glass measuring cup. Heat to between 110°F and 120°F; add 2 teaspoons of agave nectar and yeast and stir to combine. Cover and set aside for a few minutes.
3. Combine the egg, olive oil, remaining agave, and vinegar in another mixing bowl; add yeast and milk mixture. Pour wet ingredients into the bottom of your bread maker.
4. Top with dry ingredients.
5. Select Gluten-Free cycle, light color crust, and press Start.
6. After second kneading cycle sprinkle with poppy seeds.
7. Remove pan from bread machine. Leave the loaf in the pan for about 5 minutes before cooling on a rack.
8. Enjoy!

Nutrition Info: Calories: 153, Sodium: 346 mg, Dietary Fiber: 4.1 g, Fat: 5.9 g, Carbs: 24.5 g, Protein: 3.3 g.

Gluten-free Oat & Honey Bread

Servings: 12
Cooking Time: 3 Hours

Ingredients:
- 1 1/4 cups warm water
- 3 tablespoons honey
- 2 eggs
- 3 tablespoons butter, melted
- 1 1/4 cups gluten-free oats
- 1 1/4 cups brown rice flour
- 1/2 cup potato starch
- 2 teaspoons xanthan gum
- 1 1/2 teaspoons sugar
- 3/4 teaspoon salt
- 1 1/2 tablespoons active dry yeast

Directions:
1. Add ingredients in the order listed above, except for yeast.
2. Make a well in the center of the dry ingredients and add the yeast.
3. Select Gluten-Free cycle, light crust color, and press Start.
4. Remove bread and allow the bread to cool on its side on a cooling rack for 20 minutes before slicing to serve.

Nutrition Info: Calories: 151, Sodium: 265 mg, Dietary Fiber: 4.3 g, Fat: 4.5 g, Carbs: 27.2 g, Protein: 3.5 g.

Paleo Bread

Servings: 16
Cooking Time: 3 Hours 15 Minutes

Ingredients:
- 4 tablespoons chia seeds
- 1 tablespoon flax meal
- 3/4 cup, plus 1 tablespoon water
- 1/4 cup coconut oil
- 3 eggs, room temperature
- 1/2 cup almond milk
- 1 tablespoon honey
- 2 cups almond flour
- 1 1/4 cups tapioca flour
- 1/3 cup coconut flour
- 1 teaspoon salt
- 1/4 cup flax meal
- 2 teaspoons cream of tartar
- 1 teaspoon baking soda
- 2 teaspoons active dry yeast

Directions:
1. Combine the chia seeds and tablespoon of flax meal in a mixing bowl; stir in the water and set aside.
2. Melt the coconut oil in a microwave-safe dish, and let it cool down to lukewarm.
3. Whisk in the eggs, almond milk and honey.
4. Whisk in the chia seeds and flax meal gel and pour it into the bread maker pan.

5. Stir the almond flour, tapioca flour, coconut flour, salt and 1/4 cup of flax meal together.
6. Mix the cream of tartar and baking soda in a separate bowl and combine it with the other dry ingredients.
7. Pour the dry ingredients into the bread machine.
8. Make a little well on top and add the yeast.
9. Start the machine on the Wheat cycle, light or medium crust color, and press Start.
10. Remove to cool completely before slicing to serve.
Nutrition Info: Calories: 190, Sodium: 243 mg, Dietary Fiber: 5.2 g, Fat: 10.3 g, Carbs: 20.4 g, Protein: 4.5 g.

Gluten-free Pizza Crust

Servings: 6 - 8
Cooking Time: 2 Hours
Ingredients:
- 3 large eggs, room temperature
- 1/2 cup olive oil
- 1 cup milk
- 1/2 cup water
- 2 cups rice flour
- 1 cup cornstarch, and extra for dusting
- 1/2 cup potato starch
- 1/2 cup sugar
- 2 tablespoons yeast
- 3 teaspoons xanthan gum
- 1 teaspoon salt

Directions:
1. Combine the wet ingredients in a separate bowl and pour into the bread maker pan.
2. Combine the dry ingredients except yeast and add to pan.
3. Make a well in the center of the dry ingredients and add the yeast.
4. Select Dough cycle and press Start.
5. When dough is finished, press it out on a surface lightly sprinkled with corn starch and create a pizza shape. Use this dough with your favorite toppings and pizza recipe!
Nutrition Info: Calories: 463, Sodium: 547 mg, Dietary Fiber: 8.1 g, Fat: 15.8 g, Carbs: 79.2 g, Protein: 7.4 g.

Rosemary Bread

Servings: 8 Pcs
Cooking Time: 1 Hour
Ingredients:
- 300ml (1 ¼ cups) warm water
- 60ml (¼ cup) olive oil
- Two egg whites
- One tablespoon apple cider vinegar
- ½ teaspoon baking powder
- Two teaspoons dry active yeast

- Two tablespoons granulated sugar
- ½ teaspoon Italian seasoning
- ¼ teaspoon ground black pepper
- 1¼ teaspoon dried rosemary
- 200g (2 cups) gluten-free almond flour / or any other gluten-free flour, levelled
- 100g (1 cup) Tapioca/potato starch, levelled
- Two teaspoons Xanthan Gum
- One teaspoon salt

Directions:
1. According to your bread machine manufacturer, place all the ingredients into the bread machine's greased pan.
2. Select basic cycle / standard cycle/bake / quick bread / white bread setting
3. then choose crust color either medium or Light and press start to bake bread.
4. In the last kneading cycle, check the dough
5. it should be wet but thick, not like traditional bread dough. If the dough is too wet, put more flour, one tablespoon at a time, or until dough slightly firm.
6. When the cycle is finished, and the baker machine turns off, remove baked bread from pan and cool on wire rack.

Nutrition Info: Calories: 150 Calories;Total fat: 3 g ;Cholesterol: 5 mg;Sodium: 290 mg ;Carbohydrates: 24 g;Fibre: 1 g ;Protein: 6 g

Flax And Sunflower Seeds Bread

Servings: 8 Pcs
Cooking Time: 1 Hour
Ingredients:
- 300ml (1 ¼ cups) warm water
- 60ml (¼ cup) olive oil
- Two egg whites
- One tablespoon apple cider vinegar
- ½ teaspoon baking powder
- 7g (2 teaspoons) dry active yeast
- Two tablespoons granulated sugar
- 200g (2 cups) gluten-free almond flour / or any other gluten-free flour, levelled
- 100g (1 cup) Tapioca/potato starch, levelled
- Two teaspoons Xanthan Gum
- One teaspoon salt
- 55g (½ cup) flax seeds
- 55g (½ cup) sunflower seeds

Directions:
1. According to your bread machine manufacturer, place all the ingredients into the bread machine's greased pan except sunflower seeds.
2. Select basic cycle / standard cycle/bake / quick bread / white bread setting
3. then select crust colour either medium or light and press start.
4. In the last kneading cycle, check the dough
5. it should be wet but thick, not like traditional bread dough. If the dough is too wet, put more flour, one tablespoon at a time, or until dough slightly firm.

6. Add sunflower seeds 5 minutes before the kneading cycle ends.

7. When the cycle is finished and the machine turns off, remove baked bread from pan and cool on wire rack.

Nutrition Info: Calories: 90 Calories;Total fat: 2g;Cholesterol: 5 mg;Sodium: 180 mg;Carbohydrates: 18 g;Fibre: 2 g;Protein: 4 g

Gluten-free Pull-apart Rolls

Servings: 9
Cooking Time: 2 Hours
Ingredients:
- 1 cup warm water
- 2 tablespoons butter, unsalted
- 1 egg, room temperature
- 1 teaspoon apple cider vinegar
- 2 3/4 cups gluten-free almond-blend flour
- 1 1/2 teaspoons xanthan gum
- 1/4 cup sugar
- 1 teaspoon salt
- 2 teaspoons active dry yeast

Directions:
1. Add wet ingredients to the bread maker pan.
2. Mix dry ingredients except for yeast, and put in pan.
3. Make a well in the center of the dry ingredients and add the yeast.
4. Select Dough cycle and press Start.
5. Spray an 8-inch round cake pan with non-stick cooking spray.
6. When Dough cycle is complete, roll dough out into 9 balls, place in cake pan, and baste each with warm water.
7. Cover with a towel and let rise in a warm place for 1 hour.
8. Preheat oven to 400°F.
9. Bake for 26 to 28 minutes; until golden brown.
10. Brush with butter and serve.

Nutrition Info: Calories: 568, Sodium: 380 mg, Dietary Fiber: 5.5 g, Fat: 10.5 g, Carbs: 116.3 g, Protein: 8.6 g.

Grain-free Chia Bread

Servings: 12
Cooking Time: 3 Hours
Ingredients:
- 1 cup warm water
- 3 large organic eggs, room temperature
- 1/4 cup olive oil
- 1 tablespoon apple cider vinegar
- 1 cup gluten-free chia seeds, ground to flour
- 1 cup almond meal flour
- 1/2 cup potato starch

- 1/4 cup coconut flour
- 3/4 cup millet flour
- 1 tablespoon xanthan gum
- 1 1/2 teaspoons salt
- 2 tablespoons sugar
- 3 tablespoons nonfat dry milk
- 6 teaspoons instant yeast

Directions:
1. Whisk wet ingredients together and add to the bread maker pan.
2. Whisk dry ingredients, except yeast, together and add on top of wet ingredients.
3. Make a well in the dry ingredients and add yeast.
4. Select Whole Wheat cycle, light crust color, and press Start.
5. Allow to cool completely before serving.

Nutrition Info: Calories: 375, Sodium: 462 mg, Dietary Fiber: 22.3 g, Fat: 18.3 g, Carbs: 42 g, Protein: 12.2 g.

Gluten-free Simple Sandwich Bread

Servings: 12
Cooking Time: 1 Hour
Ingredients:
- 1 1/2 cups sorghum flour
- 1 cup tapioca starch or potato starch (not potato flour!)
- 1/2 cup gluten-free millet flour or gluten-free oat flour
- 2 teaspoons xanthan gum
- 1 1/4 teaspoons fine sea salt
- 2 1/2 teaspoons gluten-free yeast for bread machines
- 1 1/4 cups warm water
- 3 tablespoons extra virgin olive oil
- 1 tablespoon honey or raw agave nectar
- 1/2 teaspoon mild rice vinegar or lemon juice
- 2 organic free-range eggs, beaten

Directions:
1. Whisk together the dry ingredients except the yeast and set aside.
2. Add the liquid ingredients to the bread maker pan first, then gently pour the mixed dry ingredients on top of the liquid.
3. Make a well in the center of the dry ingredients and add the yeast.
4. Set for Rapid 1 hour 20 minutes, medium crust color, and press Start.
5. Transfer to a cooling rack for 15 minutes before slicing to serve.

Nutrition Info: Calories: 137, Sodium: 85 mg, Dietary Fiber: 2.7 g, Fat: 4.6 g, Carbs: 22.1 g, Protein: 2.4 g.

Sorghum Bread Recipe

Servings: 12
Cooking Time: 3 Hours
Ingredients:

- 1 1/2 cups sorghum flour
- 1 cup tapioca starch
- 1/2 cup brown or white sweet rice flour
- 1 teaspoon xanthan gum
- 1 teaspoon guar gum
- 1/2 teaspoon salt
- 3 tablespoons sugar
- 2 1/4 teaspoons instant yeast
- 3 eggs (room temperature, lightly beaten)
- 1/4 cup oil
- 1 1/2 teaspoons vinegar
- 3/4-1 cup milk (105 - 115°F)

Directions:
1. Combine the dry ingredients in a mixing bowl, except for yeast.
2. Add the wet ingredients to the bread maker pan, then add the dry ingredients on top.
3. Make a well in the center of the dry ingredients and add the yeast.
4. Set to Basic bread cycle, light crust color, and press Start.
5. Remove and lay on its side to cool on a wire rack before serving.

Nutrition Info: Calories: 169, Sodium: 151 mg, Dietary Fiber: 2.5 g, Fat: 6.3 g, Carbs: 25.8 g, Protein: 3.3 g.

BREAD FROM AROUND THE WORLD

Classic French Bread

Servings: 1 Pound Loaf
Cooking Time: 3 Hours
Ingredients:
- Lukewarm water :1 cup
- Sugar :2 tsp
- Salt :1 tsp
- Plain bread flour :3 ¼ cups
- Bread machine yeast :1 tsp

Directions:
1. Add the ingredients into the bread machine as per the order of the ingredients listed above or follow your bread machine's instruction manual.
2. Select the French setting and medium crust function.
3. When ready, turn the bread out onto a drying rack and allow it to cool, then serve.

Nutrition Info: (Per Serving):Calories: 206 kcal / Total fat: 0.6 g / Saturated fat: 0.1 g / Cholesterol: 0 mg Total carbohydrates: 43.4 g / Dietary fiber: 1.8 g Sodium: 292.2 mg / Protein: 5.9 g

Paleo Coconut Bread

Servings: 10 Pcs
Cooking Time: 50 Minutes
Ingredients:
- ½ cup coconut flour
- ¼ cup almond milk (unsweetened)
- ¼ cup coconut oil (melted)
- 6 eggs
- ¼ tsp. baking soda
- ¼ tsp. salt

Directions:
1. Preheat the oven to 350F.
2. Prepare a (8 x 4) bread pan with parchment paper.
3. In a bowl, combine salt, baking soda, and coconut flour.
4. Combine the oil, milk, and eggs in another bowl.
5. Gradually add the wet ingredients into the dry ingredients and mix well.
6. Pour the mixture into the prepared pan.
7. Bake for 40 to 50 minutes.
8. Cool, slice, and serve.

Nutrition Info: Calories: 108;Fat: 8.7g;Carb: 3.4g;Protein: 4.2g

White Chocolate Bread

Servings: 1 Loaf
Cooking Time: 2 Hours And 55 Minutes
Ingredients:

- ¼ cup warm water
- 1 cup warm milk
- 1 egg
- ¼ cup butter, softened
- 3 cups bread flour
- 2 tablespoons brown sugar
- 2 tablespoons white sugar
- 1 teaspoon salt
- 1 teaspoon ground cinnamon
- 1 (.25 ounce) package active dry yeast
- 1 cup white chocolate chips

Directions:
1. Place all ingredients (except the white chocolate chips) in the pan of the bread machine in the order recommended by the manufacturer.
2. Select cycle; press Start.
3. If your machine has a Fruit setting, add the white chocolate chips at the signal, otherwise you can do it about 5 minutes before the kneading cycle has finished.

Nutrition Info: Calories 277 ;Protein 6.6g;Carbohydrates 39g;Fat: 10.5g

Za'atar Bread

Servings: 12 - 14
Cooking Time: 3 Hours
Ingredients:
- 1/3 cup za'atar seasoning
- 2 tablespoons onion powder
- 1 cup warm water
- 2 tablespoons agave nectar
- 1/4 cup applesauce
- 3 cups bread flour
- 1 teaspoon salt
- 2 1/4 teaspoons rapid rise yeast

Directions:
1. Mix dry ingredients together in a bowl, except for yeast.
2. Add wet ingredients to bread pan first; top with dry ingredients.
3. Make a well in the center of the dry ingredients and add the yeast.
4. Press Basic bread cycle, choose medium crust color, and press Start.
5. Remove from bread pan and allow to cool before serving.

Nutrition Info: Calories: 125, Sodium: 196 mg, Dietary Fiber: 2 g, Fat: 1.2 g, Carbs: 24.6 g, Protein: 4.1 g

German Rye Bread

Servings: 20
Cooking Time: 3 Hour And 48 Minutes
Ingredients:
- Buttermilk – 1 ½ cups

- Whole wheat flour – 2 ½ cups
- Rye flour – ½ cup
- Bread flour – ½ cup
- Buckwheat flour – ¼ cup
- Wheat germ – ¼ cup
- Salt - 1 tsp.
- Flax seeds – ¼ cup
- Soft butter – 1 tbsp.
- Molasses – 3 tbsp.
- Active dry yeast – 3 tsp.

Directions:
1. Add everything according to the bread machine recommendations.
2. Select Whole Grain and Dark crust.
3. Remove the bread when done.
4. Cool, slice, and serve.

Nutrition Info: (Per Serving): Calories: 151; Total Fat: 4 g; Saturated Fat: 2.3 g; Carbohydrates: 23.8 g; Cholesterol: 10 mg; Fiber: 2.4 g; Calcium: 93 mg; Sodium: 193 mg; Protein: 5.6 g

Seeded Whole Wheat Bread

Servings: 1 Pound Loaf
Cooking Time: 3 Hours
Ingredients:
- Lukewarm water :⅔ cups
- Milk powder :3 tbsp
- Honey :1 tbsp
- Unsalted butter, softened :1 tbsp
- Plain bread flour :1 cup
- Whole wheat flour :1 cup
- Poppy seeds :2 tbsp
- Sesame seeds :2 tbsp
- Sunflower seeds :2 tbsp
- Salt :¾ tsp
- Instant dry yeast :2 tsp

Directions:
1. Add the ingredients into the bread machine as per the order of the ingredients listed above or follow your bread machine's instruction manual.
2. Select the basic setting and medium crust function.
3. When ready, turn the bread out onto a drying rack and allow it to cool, then serve.

Nutrition Info: (Per Serving):Calories: 84 kcal / Total fat: 2 g / Saturated fat: 1 g / Cholesterol: 2 mg / Total carbohydrates: 14 g / Dietary fiber: 1 g Sodium: 133 mg / Protein: 3 g

Almond Banana Pancakes

Servings: 4 Pcs
Cooking Time: 10 Minutes
Ingredients:

- 1 Ripe Banana, mashed
- 4 Eggs
- 1/2 cup Almond Flour
- 2 tbsp Erythritol
- 1 tsp Baking Powder
- 1 tsp Ground Cinnamon

Directions:
1. Whisk together almond flour, baking powder, and cinnamon in a bowl.
2. In a separate bowl, mix mashed banana, eggs, and erythritol.
3. Gradually fold in the dry ingredients until becoming a wet mixture.
4. Preheat a skillet and coat with non-stick spray.
5. Spoon in the batter and cook for 1-2 minutes per side.

Nutrition Info: Kcal per serve: 235;Fat: 17 g. (64%);Protein: 11 g. (21%);Carbs: 10 g. (16%)

Puri Bread

Servings: 6 Pcs
Cooking Time: 5 Minutes
Ingredients:
- 1 cup almond flour, sifted
- ½ cup of warm water
- 2 Tbsp. clarified butter
- 1 cup olive oil for frying
- Salt to taste

Directions:
1. Salt the water and add the flour.
2. Make some holes in the center of the dough and pour warm clarified butter.
3. Knead the dough and let stand for 15 minutes, covered.
4. Shape into six balls.
5. Flatten the balls into six thin rounds using a rolling pin.
6. Heat enough oil to cover a round frying pan completely.
7. Place a puri in it when hot.
8. Fry for 20 seconds on each side.
9. Place on a paper towel.
10. Repeat with the rest of the puri and serve.

Nutrition Info: Calories: 106;Fat: 3g;Carb: 6g;Protein: 3g

Zesty Poppy Seed Bread

Servings: 1 Loaf
Cooking Time: 1 Hour And 30 Minutes
Ingredients:
- 9.5 ounces almond flour
- Two lemons, zest only
- ½ cup no-calorie sweetener of your choice
- Three tablespoons butter
- Two tablespoons poppy seeds

- ½ teaspoon baking powder
- Six eggs
- Two tablespoons lemon juice
- Two tablespoons water

Directions:
1. Put the wet ingredients, followed by the dry ingredients, into the bread pan.
2. Select the "Quick" or "Cake" mode of your bread machine.
3. Allow the cycles to be completed.
4. Remove the bread pan from the machine but keep the bread in the container for another 10 minutes.
5. Take out the bread from the bread pan, and let it cool down completely before slicing.

Nutrition Info: Calories: 70;Carbohydrates: 6g;Fat: 17g;Protein: 9g

European Black Bread

Servings: 1 Loaf
Cooking Time: 1 Hour And 5 Minutes
Ingredients:
- ¾ teaspoon cider vinegar
- 1 cup of water
- ½ cup rye flour
- 1 ½ cups flour
- One tablespoon margarine
- ¼ cup of oat bran
- One teaspoon salt
- 1 ½ tablespoons sugar
- One teaspoon dried onion flakes
- One teaspoon caraway seed
- One teaspoon yeast
- Two tablespoons unsweetened cocoa

Directions:
1. Put everything in your bread machine.
2. Now select the basic setting.
3. Hit the start button.
4. Transfer bread to a rack for cooling once done.

Nutrition Info: Calories 114;Carbohydrates: 22 g;Total Fat 1.7 g;Cholesterol 0mg;Protein 3 g;Sugar 2 g;Sodium 247 mg

Butter Bread

Servings: 1 Pound Loaf
Cooking Time: 3 Hours And 35 Minutes
Ingredients:
- Egg :1
- Lukewarm whole milk :1 ¼ cup
- Unsalted butter, diced :½ cup
- Plain bread flour :2 cups

- Salt :1 pinch
- Sugar :1 pinch
- Instant dry yeast :2 tsp

Directions:
1. Add the ingredients into the bread machine as per the order of the ingredients listed above or follow your bread machine's instruction manual.
2. Select the French setting and medium crust function.
3. When ready, turn the bread out onto a drying rack and allow it to cool, then serve.

Nutrition Info: (Per Serving):Calories: 262.2 kcal / Total fat: 13.5 g / Saturated fat: 8.2 g / Cholesterol: 58.6 mg / Total carbohydrates 29.8 g / Dietary fiber: 1.3 g / Sodium: 45.3 mg / Protein: 5.9 g

Italian Bread

Servings: 2 Loaves
Cooking Time: 1 Hour And 10 Minutes

Ingredients:
- One tablespoon of light brown sugar
- 4 cups all-purpose flour, unbleached
- 1 ½ teaspoon of salt
- One 1/3 cups + 1 tablespoon warm water
- One package active dry yeast
- 1 ½ teaspoon of olive oil
- One egg
- Two tablespoons cornmeal

Directions:
1. Place flour, brown sugar, 1/3 cup warm water, salt, olive oil, and yeast in your bread machine. Select the dough cycle. Hit the start button.
2. Deflate your dough. Turn it on a floured surface.
3. Form two loaves from the dough.
4. Keep them on your cutting board. The seam side should be down. Sprinkle some cornmeal on your board.
5. Place a damp cloth on your loaves to cover them.
6. Wait for 40 minutes. The volume should double.
7. In the meantime, preheat your oven to 190 °C.
8. Beat 1 tablespoon of water and an egg in a bowl.
9. Brush this mixture on your loaves.
10. Make an extended cut at the center of your loaves with a knife.
11. Shake your cutting board gently, making sure that the loaves do not stick.
12. Now slide your loaves on a baking sheet.
13. Bake in your oven for about 35 minutes.

Nutrition Info: Calories 105;Carbohydrates: 20.6 g;Total Fat 0.9 g;Cholesterol 9 mg;Protein 3.1 g;Fiber 1 g;Sugar 1g;Sodium 179 mg;Potassium 39 mg

Sour Cream Chieve Bread

Servings: 1 Loaf

Cooking Time: 3 Hours
Ingredients:
- 2/3 cup whole milk (70° to 80°)
- 1/4 cup water (70° to 80°)
- 1/4 cup sour cream
- 2 tablespoons butter
- 1-1/2 teaspoons sugar
- 1-1/2 teaspoons salt
- 3 cups bread flour
- 1/8 teaspoon baking soda
- 1/4 cup minced chives
- 2-1/4 teaspoons active dry yeast

Directions:
1. Place all the ingredients in the bread machine pan, in the order suggested by the manufacturer.
2. Select basic bread setting.
3. Choose crust coolor and loaf size if available.
4. Bake according to bread machine directions
5. Check the dough after 5 minutes of mixing and add 1 or 2 tablespoons of water or flour if needed.

Nutrition Info: Calories 105;Fat 2g;Saturated fat 2g;Cholesterol 8mg;Sodium 253mg;Carbohydrate 18g;Protein 4g

Simple Dark Rye Bread

Servings: 1 Loaf (8 Slices)
Cooking Time: 2 Hours
Ingredients:
- 2/3 cup lukewarm water (80 degrees F)
- One tablespoon melted butter cooled
- ¼ cup molasses
- ¼ teaspoon salt
- One tablespoon unsweetened cocoa powder
- ½ cup rye flour
- pinch of ground nutmeg
- 1¼ cups white wheat flour sifted
- 1 1/8 teaspoons active dry yeast

Directions:
1. Prepare all of the ingredients for your bread and measuring means (a cup, a spoon, kitchen scales).
2. Carefully measure the ingredients into the pan.
3. Place all of the ingredients into the bread bucket in the right order and follow your bread machine's manual.
4. Close the cover.
5. Select the program of your bread machine to BASIC and choose the crust colour to MEDIUM.
6. Wait until the program completes.
7. When done, take the bucket out and let it cool for 5-10 minutes.

8. Shake the loaf from the pan and let cool for 30 minutes on a cooling rack.
9. Slice, serve and enjoy the taste of fragrant homemade bread.
Nutrition Info: Calories 151;Total Fat 2.1g;Saturated Fat 1g;Cholesterol 4g;Sodium 88mg;Total Carbohydrate 29.4g;Dietary Fiber 2.7g;Total Sugars 5.9g;Protein 4.2g

Apple Cake

Servings: 10
Cooking Time: 3 Hours
Ingredients:
- ● ⅔ cup water
- ● 3 tbsp unsalted butter, softened
- ● 2 cups plain bread flour
- ● 3 tbsp granulated sugar
- ● 1 tsp salt
- ● 1 ½ tsp active dry yeast
- ● 1 can apple pie filling

Directions:
1. Add the ingredients into the bread machine as per the order of the ingredients listed above or follow your bread machine's instruction manual. Do not add the pie filling.
2. Select the dough setting.
3. Remove the dough and place it onto a floured surface. Cover with a cotton cloth for 15 minutes.
4. Roll the dough out into an even rectangular shape 13" x 8". Transfer this onto a greased baking tray. Fill the dough with the apple filling, running lengthwise. On each 13-inch side, make cuts from filling to edge of dough at 1-inch intervals, using a sharp knife. Fold ends of the dough up over the filling. Fold strips diagonally over filling, overlapping in the center and alternating sides. Cover again with the cloth and allow to rest for 30 minutes or until the dough has doubled in size.
5. Preheat your oven to 375 °F and bake the cake for 40 minutes or until it has reached a beautiful golden color.
6. When ready, turn the apple cake out onto a drying rack and allow it to cool.
7. When cooled, dust with powdered sugar and serve.
Nutrition Info: (Per Serving):Calories: 480 kcal / Total fat: 10 g / Saturated fat: 5 g / Cholesterol: 25 mg / Total carbohydrates: 92 g / Dietary fiber: 3 g / Sodium: 710 mg / Protein: 8 g

Low-carb Keto Bread

Servings: 1 Pound Loaf
Cooking Time: 3 Hours
Ingredients:
- Oat fiber :¼ cup
- Flaxseed meal :⅓ cup
- Wheat gluten :½ cup
- Salt :½ tsp
- Xylitol :⅛ cup

- Xanthan gum :¼ tsp
- Lukewarm water :½ cup
- Egg :1
- Honey :½ tsp
- Unsalted butter, softened :1 tbsp
- Active dry yeast :½ tbsp

Directions:

1. In a mixing bowl, combine the oat fiber, meal, gluten, salt, xylitol, and xanthan gum.
2. Add the water, egg, honey, and butter into the bread machine, followed by the oat fiber mixture and yeast.
3. Select the basic setting and soft crust function.
4. When ready, turn the bread out onto a drying rack and allow it to cool, then serve.

Nutrition Info: (Per Serving):Calories: 122 kcal / Total fat: 5.4 g / Saturated fat: 1.4 g / Cholesterol: 72 mg / Total carbohydrates: 6.5 g / Dietary fiber: 2.4 g / Sodium: 158 mg / Protein: 13.3 g

Swedish Cardamom Bread

Servings: 1 Loaf
Cooking Time: 15 Minutes
Ingredients:

- ¼ cup of sugar
- ¾ cup of warm milk
- ¾ teaspoon cardamom
- ½ teaspoon salt
- ¼ cup of softened butter
- One egg
- Two ¼ teaspoons bread machine yeast
- 3 cups all-purpose flour
- Five tablespoons milk for brushing
- Two tablespoons sugar for sprinkling

Directions:

1. Put everything (except milk for brushing and sugar for sprinkling) in the pan of your bread machine.
2. Select the dough cycle. Hit the start button. You should have an elastic and smooth dough once the process is complete. It should be double in size.
3. Transfer to a lightly floured surface.
4. Now divide into three balls. Set aside for 10 minutes.
5. Roll all the balls into long ropes of around 14 inches.
6. Braid the shapes. Pinch ends under securely and keeps on a cookie sheet. You can also divide your dough into two balls. Smooth them and keep on your bread pan.
7. Brush milk over the braid. Sprinkle sugar lightly.
8. Now bake in your oven for 25 minutes at 375 degrees F (190 degrees C).
9. Take a foil and cover for the final 10 minutes. It's prevents over-browning.
10. Transfer to your cooling rack.

Nutrition Info: Calories 135;Carbohydrates: 22g;Total Fat 7g;Cholesterol 20mg;Protein 3g;Fiber 1g;Sugar 3g;Sodium 100mg

Paleo And Dairy-free Bread

Servings: 1 Pound Loaf
Cooking Time: 3 Hours
Ingredients:
- Flax meal :¼ cup
- Chia seeds :2 tbsp
- Coconut oil, melted :⅛ cup
- Egg :1 ½
- Almond milk :¼ cup
- Honey :½ tbsp
- Almond flour :1 cup
- Tapioca flour :⅔ cup
- Coconut flour :⅛ cup
- Salt :½ tsp
- Cream of tartar :1 tsp
- Bread machine yeast :1 tsp

Directions:
1. In a mixing bowl, combine one tablespoon of flax meal with the chia seeds. Stir in the water and set aside.
2. In a separate mixing bowl, pour in the melted coconut oil, eggs, almond milk, and honey. Whisk together. Followed by whisking in the flax meal and chia seed mixture. Pour this into the bread machine.
3. In a mixing bowl, combine the almond, tapioca, and coconut flour. Add the remainder of the flax meal and salt. Add in the cream of tartar and baking soda.
4. Pour the dry ingredients on top of the wet ingredients.
5. Finish by adding the yeast.
6. Select the whole wheat setting and medium crust function.
7. When ready, turn the bread out onto a drying rack and allow it to cool, then serve.

Nutrition Info: (Per Serving):Calories: 142 kcal / Total fat: 6.3 g / Saturated fat: 1.8g / Cholesterol: 34.9 mg / Total carbohydrates: 15.5 g / Dietary fiber: 4.4 g / Sodium: 236.8 mg / Protein: 4.1 g

Portugese Sweet Bread

Servings: 1 Loaf
Cooking Time: 3 Hours
Ingredients:
- 1 cup milk
- 1 egg
- 2 tablespoons margarine
- ⅓ cup white sugar
- ¾ teaspoon salt
- 3 cups bread flour
- 2 ½ teaspoons active dry yeast

Directions:

1. Add ingredients in order suggested by your manufacturer.
2. Select "sweet bread" setting.

Nutrition Info: Calories 56 ;Protein 1.5g;Carbohydrates 6.9g;Fat: 2.6g

Sausage Bread

Servings: 10
Cooking Time: 3 Hours And 25 Minutes
Ingredients:
- Bread machine yeast – 1 tsp.
- Wheat bread machine flour – 3 ½ cups
- Kosher salt – 1 tsp.
- Sugar – 1 tbsp.
- Olive oil – 1 ½ tbsp.
- Smoked sausage – 2 tbsp., chopped into small cubes
- Grated cheddar cheese – 2 tbsp., grated
- Garlic – 1 tbsp., crushed
- Lukewarm water – 1 cup

Directions:
1. Add everything (except the sausage) in the bread machine according to bread machine recommendations.
2. Select Basic cycle and Medium crust.
3. Add the sausage after the beep.
4. Remove the bread when done.
5. Cool, slice and serve.

Nutrition Info: (Per Serving): Calories: 260; Total Fat: 5.6 g; Saturated Fat: 1.4 g; Carbohydrates: 43.8 g; Cholesterol: 8 mg; Fiber: 1.6 g; Calcium: 55 mg; Sodium: 355 mg; Protein: 7.7 g

Keto Coconut Bread

Servings: 1 Loaf
Cooking Time: 1 Hour And 30 Minutes
Ingredients:
- ½ cup coconut flour
- ½ cup ground flaxseed
- Two tablespoons no-calorie sweetener of your choice
- One tablespoon baking powder
- One teaspoon xanthan gum
- ½ teaspoon ground cinnamon
- ½ teaspoon salt
- Six eggs
- 1/3 cup coconut milk
- 1/3 cup coconut oil

Directions:
1. Put all the wet ingredients first into the bread pan before adding the dry ingredients.
2. Press the "Quick" or "Cake" setting of your bread machine.
3. Remove the pan from the machine once all cycles are finished.

4. Keep the bread in the pan for ten more minutes.
5. Take out the bread on the pan and let it cool down.
6. Slice and serve.

Nutrition Info: Calories: 122;Carbohydrates: 4g;Fat: 9g;Protein: 4g

Peanut Butter And Jelly Bread

Servings: 1 Loaf
Cooking Time: 1 Hour And 10 Minutes
Ingredients:
- 1 1/2 tablespoons vegetable oil
- 1 cup of water
- ½ cup blackberry jelly
- ½ cup peanut butter
- One teaspoon salt
- One tablespoon white sugar
- 2 cups of bread flour
- 1 cup whole-wheat flour
- 1 1/2 teaspoons active dry yeast

Directions:
1. Put everything in your bread machine pan.
2. Select the basic setting.
3. Press the start button.
4. Take out the pan when done and set aside for 10 minutes.

Nutrition Info: Calories: 153 Cal;Carbohydrates: 20 g;Fat: 9g;Cholesterol: 0mg;Protein: 4g;Fiber: 2g ;Sugar: 11g;Sodium: 244mg;Potassium: 120mg

Greek Bread

Servings: 18
Cooking Time: 3 Hours And 25 Minutes
Ingredients:
- Milk – 1 cup
- Crumbled feta cheese – ½ cup
- Chopped pitted kalamata olives – 1/3 cup
- Water – 2 tbsp.
- Oil – 2 tsp.
- Bread flour – 3 cups
- Sugar – 1 tbsp.
- Dried rosemary – 1 tsp., crushed
- Salt – ½ tsp.
- Active dry yeast – 1 tsp.

Directions:
1. Add everything in the bread machine according to bread machine recommendations.
2. Select Basic White bread cycle.
3. Remove the bread when done.
4. Cool, slice, and serve.

Nutrition Info: (Per Serving): Calories: 110; Total Fat: 2 g; Saturated Fat: 0.5 g; Carbohydrates: 18 g; Cholesterol: 4 mg; Fiber: 1 g; Calcium: 38 mg; Sodium: 118 mg; Protein: 4 g

Low-carb Apple Bread

Servings: 1 Loaf
Cooking Time: 1 Hour And 30 Minutes
Ingredients:
- Two apples, peeled and chopped
- 2 cups almond flour
- ½ cup golden flaxseed, milled
- ½ cup no-calorie sweetener of your choice
- Two teaspoons cinnamon
- ¾ teaspoon baking soda
- ¾ teaspoon salt
- ½ teaspoon nutmeg
- Four eggs, lightly beaten
- ¼ cup of water
- ¼ cup heavy cream
- Four tablespoons coconut oil
- Two teaspoons vanilla extract
- 1 ½ teaspoon apple cider vinegar

Directions:
1. Place all ingredients in the pan according to the order specified above.
2. Set the bread machine to "Cake" or "Quick" mode.
3. Let the cycles finish.
4. Remove the bread pan from the machine, but keep the bread in the pan for another 10 minutes.
5. Slice the bread only when it has cooled down.

Nutrition Info: Calories: 242;Carbohydrates: 11g;Fat: 20g;Protein: 7g

Pita Bread With Black Cumin

Servings: 8 Pcs
Cooking Time: 15 Minutes
Ingredients:
- 2 cups almond flour, sifted
- ½ cup of water
- 2 Tbsp. olive oil
- Salt, to taste
- 1 tsp. black cumin

Directions:
1. Preheat the oven to 400F.
2. Combine the flour with salt. Add the water and olive oil.
3. Knead the dough and let stand about 15 minutes.
4. Shape the dough into eight balls.
5. Line a baking sheet with parchment paper and flatten the balls into eight thin rounds.

6. Sprinkle black cumin.
7. Bake for 15 minutes, serve.
Nutrition Info: Calories: 73;Fat: 6.9g;Carbohydrates: 1.6g;Protein: 1.6g

No-bake Butter Cookies

Servings: 8 Pcs
Cooking Time: 0 Minutes
Ingredients:
- ½ cup almond flour
- 1½ tbsp butter
- 1 tbsp Swerve
- ½ tsp vanilla extract
- 1 pinch salt

Directions:
1. Mix all the ingredients in a bowl to prepare the cookie batter.
2. Spoon out the batter onto a cookie sheet positioned on a baking tray.
3. Put the tray in the refrigerator and refrigerate for about 1 hour 10 minutes.
4. Serve the cookies.
Nutrition Info: Calories: 125 Cal;Fat: 3.2 g;Cholesterol: 11 mg;Sodium: 75 mg;Carbohydrates: 3,6 g

Ciabatta

Servings: 1 Pound Loaf
Cooking Time: 30 Minutes
Ingredients:
- Lukewarm water :¾ cup
- Extra-virgin olive oil :½ tbsp
- White all-purpose flour :1 ½ cups
- Salt :¾ tsp
- Sugar :½ tsp
- Bread machine yeast :¾ tsp

Directions:
1. Add the ingredients into the bread machine as per the order of the ingredients listed above or follow your bread machine's instruction manual.
2. Select the dough cycle.
3. When the dough is ready, place it onto a floured surface. Cover the dough with a ceramic or glass dish and allow it to rest for ten minutes.
4. Shape the dough an oval shape. Split into two oval shapes when doubling up on the recipe.
5. Place onto a greased baking tray, cover with a cloth and allow to rest for a further 30 minutes or until it has doubled in size. Allow the dough to rest in a dry, warm area of your kitchen.
6. Preheat your oven to 425 °F.
7. Using the bottom end of a wooden spoon make small indents on the top of each loaf. Drive the spoon down into the dough until it touches the baking tray. Then place into the oven and bake for 30 minutes.

8. Sprinkle water lightly over the top of the loaves every 10 minutes while baking.
9. When ready, turn the bread out onto a drying rack and allow it to cool, then serve.
Nutrition Info: (Per Serving):Calories: 190 kcal / Total fat: 2.2 g / Saturated fat: 0.3 g / Cholesterol: 0 mg / Total carbohydrates: 36.6 g / Dietary fiber: 1.4 g / Sodium: 441 mg / Protein: 5.1 g

Italian Parmesan Bread

Servings: 1 Pound Loaf
Cooking Time: 3 Hours
Ingredients:
- Lukewarm water :¾ cups
- White all-purpose flour :2 cups
- Shredded parmesan cheese :⅛ cup
- Salt :¾ tsp
- Italian mixed herbs :½ tsp
- Garlic powder :½ tsp
- Instant dry yeast :1 ¼ tsp

Directions:
1. Add the ingredients into the bread machine as per the order of the ingredients listed above or follow your bread machine's instruction manual.
2. Select the basic setting and medium crust function.
3. When ready, turn the bread out onto a drying rack and allow it to cool, then serve.
Nutrition Info: (Per Serving):Calories: 103.1 kcal / Total fat: 0.4 g / Saturated fat: 0.1 g / Cholesterol: 0.2 mg / Total carbohydrates: 21.3 g / Dietary fiber: 0.8 g / Sodium: 14.1 g / Protein: 3 g

Country-styled White Bread

Servings: 1 Pound Loaf
Cooking Time: 2 Hours And 5 Minutes
Ingredients:
- Lukewarm water :1 ½ cups
- Extra-virgin olive oil :1 ½ tbsp
- Plain bread flour :1 cup
- White all-purpose Flour :2 ½ cups
- Baking soda :¼ tsp
- Sugar :1 ½ tsp
- Salt :1 pinch
- Bread machine yeast :2 ½ tsp

Directions:
1. Add the ingredients into the bread machine as per the order of the ingredients listed above or follow your bread machine's instruction manual.
2. Select the rapid setting and the medium crust function.
3. When ready, turn the bread out onto a drying rack and allow it to cool, then serve.
Nutrition Info: (Per Serving):Calories: 122 kcal / Total fat: 5 g / Saturated fat: 1 g / Cholesterol: 0 mg / Total carbohydrates: 17 g / Dietary fiber: 2 g Sodium: 394 mg / Protein: 2 g

Healthy Low Carb Bread

Servings: 8 Slices
Cooking Time: 35 Minutes
Ingredients:
- 2/3 cup coconut flour
- 2/3 cup coconut oil (softened not melted)
- Nine eggs
- 2 tsp. Cream of tartar
- ¾ tsp. xanthan gum
- 1 tsp. Baking soda
- ¼ tsp. salt

Directions:
1. Preheat the oven to 350F.
2. Grease a loaf pan with 1 to 2 tsp. Melted coconut oil and place it in the freezer to harden.
3. Add eggs into a bowl and mix for 2 minutes with a hand mixer.
4. Add coconut oil into the eggs and mix.
5. Add dry ingredients to a second bowl and whisk until mixed.
6. Put the dry ingredients into the egg mixture and mix on low speed with a hand mixer until dough is formed and the mixture is incorporated.
7. Add the dough into the prepared loaf pan, transfer into the preheated oven, and bake for 35 minutes.
8. Take out the bread pan from the oven.
9. Cool, slice, and serve.

Nutrition Info: Calories: 229;Fat: 25.5g Carb: 6.5g;Protein: 8.5g

Sourdough

Servings: 1 Pound Loaf
Cooking Time: 3 Hours
Ingredients:
- for a sourdough starter:
- 2 cups white, all-purpose flour
- 1 tsp active dry yeast
- 2 cups lukewarm water
- for bread
- Sourdough starter :½ cup
- Lukewarm water :⅓ cup
- Sugar :½ tbsp
- Active dry yeast :½ tbsp
- Plain bread flour :1 ½ cups
- Vegetable oil :1 ½ tbsp
- Salt :1 tsp

Directions:
1. for a sourdough starter:

2. Combine the ingredients in a glass or ceramic dish. Ensure the dish is big enough to allow for expansion.
3. Cover the dish with cloth, fix the cloth into place using an elastic band.
4. Allow the starter to rest for five days in a warm area. Stir the starter once a day.
5. Your starter sourdough is now ready for use. Refrigerate the remainder and use it when needed. If you would like to make a few loaves, you can keep the sourdough starter "alive" by feeding it equal amounts of flour and water and allowing it to rest in a warm area and using it when needed.
6. for bread:
7. Add the sourdough starter, water, sugar, and yeast into the bread maker. Using a spatula, combine the ingredients.
8. Allow it to rest for ten minutes.
9. Add bread flour, oil, and salt.
10. Select the basic setting and medium crust function.
11. When ready, turn the bread out onto a drying rack and allow it to cool, then serve.

Nutrition Info: (Per Serving):Calories: 181.3 kcal / Total fat: 4.5 g / Saturated fat: 0.6 g Cholesterol: 0 mg / Total carbohydrates: 30.4 g / Dietary fiber: 1.3 g / Sodium: 467 mg / Protein: 4.4 g

Hot Dog Buns

Servings: 10 Pcs
Cooking Time: 50 Minutes
Ingredients:
- One ¼ cups almond flour
- 5 tbsp. psyllium husk powder
- 1 tsp. sea salt
- 2 tsp. baking powder
- One ¼ cups boiling water
- 2 tsp. lemon juice
- Three egg whites

Directions:
1. Preheat the oven to 350F
2. In a bowl, put all dry ingredients and mix well.
3. Add boiling water, lemon juice, and egg whites into the dry mixture and whisk until combined.
4. Mould the dough into ten portions and roll into buns.
5. Transfer into the preheated oven and cook for 40 to 50 minutes on the lower oven rack.
6. Check for doneness and remove it.
7. Top with desired toppings and hot dogs and serve.

Nutrition Info: Calories: 104;Fat: 8g;Carb: 1g;Protein: 4g

British Hot Cross Buns

Servings: 12
Cooking Time: 2 Hours 30 Minutes
Ingredients:

- 3/4 cup warm milk
- 3 tablespoons butter, unsalted
- 1/4 cup white sugar
- 1/2 teaspoon salt
- 1 egg
- 1 egg white
- 3 cups all-purpose flour
- 1 tablespoon active dry yeast
- 3/4 cup dried raisins
- 1 teaspoon ground cinnamon
- For Brushing:
- 1 egg yolk
- 2 tablespoons water
- For the Crosses:
- 2 tablespoons flour
- Cold water
- 1/2 tablespoon sugar

Directions:
1. Put milk, butter, 1/4 cup sugar, salt, egg, egg white, flour, and yeast in bread maker and start the Dough cycle.
2. Add raisins and cinnamon 5 minutes before kneading cycle ends.
3. Allow to rest in machine until doubled, about 30 minutes.
4. Punch down on a floured surface, cover, and let rest 10 minutes.
5. Shape into 12 balls and place in a greased 9-by-12-inch pan.
6. Cover and let rise in a warm place until doubled, about 35-40 minutes.
7. Mix egg yolk and 2 tablespoons water and baste each bun.
8. Mix the cross ingredients to form pastry.
9. Roll out pastry and cut into thin strips. Place across the buns to form crosses.
10. Bake at 375°F for 20 minutes.
11. Remove from pan immediately and cool on a rack. Serve warm.

Nutrition Info: Calories: 200, Sodium: 135 mg, Dietary Fiber: 1.5 g, Fat: 4 g, Carbs: 36.5 g, Protein: 5.2 g

Thin Crust Pizza Dough

Servings: 1 Pizza
Cooking Time: 1 Hour And 30 Minutes
Ingredients:
- Warm water – ¾ cup, 100ºF to 110ºF
- All-purpose flour – 2 cups
- Salt – ½ tsp.
- White sugar – ¼ tsp.
- Active dry yeast – 1 tsp.
- Olive oil 2 tsp.

Directions:
1. Add everything in the bread machine according to bread machine recommendations.
2. Select dough setting and start.

3. Transfer the dough to a well-floured work surface when done.
4. Roll the dough out into a thin crust and bake.

Nutrition Info: (Per Serving): Calories: 126.2; Total Fat: 1.5 g; Saturated Fat: 0.2 g; Carbohydrates: 24.2 g; Cholesterol: 0 mg; Fiber: 0.9 g; Calcium: 5.8 mg; Sodium: 146.9 mg; Protein: 3.4 g

Nut Bread

Servings: 1 Pound Loaf
Cooking Time: 3 Hours
Ingredients:
- Lukewarm water :⅔ cup
- Vegetable oil :½ tbsp
- Lemon juice :½ tsp
- Salt :1 tsp
- Molasses :⅙ cup
- Quick oatmeal :⅓ cup
- Whole wheat flour :½ cup
- Plain bread flour :1 ⅓ cup
- Walnuts :1 ½ cups
- Instant dry yeast :1 ½ tsp

Directions:
1. Add the ingredients into the bread machine as per the order of the ingredients listed above or follow your bread machine's instruction manual.
2. Select the basic setting and soft crust function.
3. When ready, turn the bread out onto a drying rack and allow it to cool, then serve.

Nutrition Info: (Per Serving):Calories: 163 kcal / Total fat: 6.3 g / Saturated fat: 0.5 g / Cholesterol: 0 mg / Total carbohydrates: 22.8 g / Dietary fiber: 2.3 g / Sodium: 198 mg / Protein: 5.3 g

BASIC BREAD

Anadama White Bread

Servings: 14 Slices
Cooking Time: 3 H.
Ingredients:
- 1⅛ cups water (110°F/43°C)
- ⅓ cup molasses
- 1½ Tbsp butter at room temperature
- 1 tsp salt
- ⅓ cup yellow cornmeal
- 3½ cups bread flour
- 2½ tsp bread machine yeast

Directions:
1. Add each ingredient to the bread machine in the order and at the temperature recommended by your bread machine manufacturer.
2. Close the lid, select the basic bread, low crust setting on your bread machine, and press start.
3. When the bread machine has finished baking, remove the bread and put it on a cooling rack.

Whole Wheat Rolls

Servings: 12
Cooking Time: 3 Hours
Ingredients:
- 1 tablespoon sugar
- 1 teaspoon salt
- 2 3/4 cups whole wheat flour
- 2 teaspoons dry active yeast
- 1/4 cup water
- 1 egg
- 7/8 cup milk
- 1/4 cup butter

Directions:
1. All ingredients should be brought to room temperature before baking.
2. Add the wet ingredients to the bread maker pan.
3. Measure and add the dry ingredients (except yeast) to the pan.
4. Make a well in the center of the dry ingredients and add the yeast.
5. Carefully place the yeast in the hole.
6. Select the Dough cycle, then press Start.
7. Divide dough into 12 portions and shape them into balls.
8. Preheat an oven to 350°F. Place rolls on a greased baking pan.
9. Bake for 25 to 30 minutes, until golden brown.
10. Butter and serve warm.

Nutrition Info: Calories: 147, Sodium: 236 mg, Dietary Fiber: 3.5 g, Fat: 5.1 g, Carbs: 22.1 g, Protein: 5.1 g.

Orange Date Bread

Servings: 1 Loaf
Cooking Time: 1 Hour And 30 Minutes
Ingredients:
- 2 cups all-purpose flour
- 1 cup dates, chopped
- ¾ cup of sugar
- ½ cup walnuts, chopped
- Two tablespoons orange rind, grated
- 1 ½ teaspoons baking powder
- One teaspoon baking soda
- ½ cup of orange juice
- ½ cup of water
- One tablespoon vegetable oil
- One teaspoon vanilla extract

Directions:
1. Put the wet ingredients then the dry ingredients into the bread pan.
2. Press the "Quick" or "Cake" mode of the bread machine.
3. Allow all cycles to be finished.
4. Remove the pan from the machine, but keep the bread in the pan for 10 minutes more.
5. Take out the bread from the pan, and let it cool down completely before slicing.

Nutrition Info: Calories: 80;Carbohydrates: 14g;Fat: 2g;Protein: 1g

Perfect Cocoa Bread

Servings: 10
Cooking Time: 3 Hours
Ingredients:
- Milk – 1 cup.
- Egg – 1
- Egg yolk – 1
- Olive oil – 3 tbsps.
- Vanilla extract – 1 tsp.
- Salt – 1 tsp.
- Bread flour – 3 cups.
- Brown sugar – ½ cup.
- Cocoa powder – 1/3 cup.
- Vital wheat gluten – 1 tbsp.
- Yeast – 2 ½ tsps.

Directions:
1. Add all ingredients into the bread machine pan. Select basic setting then select medium crust and start. Once loaf is done, remove the loaf pan from the machine. Allow it to cool for 10 minutes. Slice and serve.

Classic White Bread I

Servings: 1 Loaf
Cooking Time: 10 Minutes
Ingredients:
- 16 slice bread (2 pounds)
- 1½ cups lukewarm water
- 1 tablespoon + 1 teaspoon olive oil
- 1½ teaspoons sugar
- 1 teaspoon table salt
- ¼ teaspoon baking soda
- 2½ cups all-purpose flour
- 1 cup white bread flour
- 2½ teaspoons bread machine yeast

Directions:
1. Preparing the Ingredients
2. Choose the size of bread to prepare. Measure and add the ingredients to the pan in the order as indicated in the ingredient listing. Place the pan in the bread machine and close the lid.
3. Select the Bake cycle
4. Close the lid, Turn on the bread maker. Select the White / Basic setting, then select the dough size and crust color. Press start to start the cycle.
5. When this is done, and the bread is baked, remove the pan from the machine. Let stand a few minutes.
6. Remove the bread from the pan and leave it on a wire rack to cool for at least 10 minutes.
7. After this time, proceed to cut it

Whole Wheat Breakfast Bread

Servings: 14 Slices
Cooking Time: 3 H. 5 Min.
Ingredients:
- 3 cups white whole wheat flour
- ½ tsp salt
- 1 cup water
- ½ cup coconut oil, liquified
- 4 Tbsp honey
- 2½ tsp active dry yeast

Directions:
1. Add each ingredient to the bread machine in the order and at the temperature recommended by your bread machine manufacturer.
2. Close the lid, select the basic bread, medium crust setting on your bread machine and press start.
3. When the bread machine has finished baking, remove the bread and put it on a cooling rack.

Homemade Wonderful Bread

Servings: 2 Loaves
Cooking Time: 15 Minutes

Ingredients:

- 2 1/2 teaspoons active dry yeast
- 1/4 cup warm water
- One tablespoon white sugar
- 4 cups all-purpose flour
- 1/4 cup dry potato flakes
- 1/4 cup dry milk powder
- Two teaspoons salt
- 1/4 cup white sugar
- Two tablespoons margarine
- 1 cup of warm water(45 degrees C)

Directions:

1. Prepare the yeast, 1/4 cup warm water and sugar to whisk and then let it sit in 15 minutes.
2. Take all ingredients together with yeast mixture to put in the pan of bread machine according to the manufacturer's recommended order. Choose basic and light crust settings.

Nutrition Info: Calories: 162 calories;Total Carbohydrate: 31.6 g ;Cholesterol: < 1 mg ;Total Fat: 1.8 g ;Protein: 4.5 g

Friendship Bread

Servings: 12
Cooking Time: 3 Hours 10 Minutes

Ingredients:

- 1 cup Amish Friendship Bread Starter
- 3 eggs
- 2/3 cup vegetable oil
- 1/4 cup milk
- 1 cup sugar
- 1/2 teaspoon vanilla extract
- 2 teaspoons cinnamon
- 1 1/2 teaspoons baking powder
- 1/2 teaspoon salt
- 1/2 teaspoon baking soda
- 2 cups flour
- 2 small boxes instant vanilla pudding

Directions:

1. Add all of the wet ingredients into the bread maker pan.
2. Add in dry ingredients, except sugar and cinnamon.
3. Set bread machine on Sweet cycle, light crust color and press Start.
4. During the last 30 minutes of baking, lift lid and quickly add 1/4 cup sugar and 1/4 teaspoon of cinnamon.
5. When finished baking, leave in bread machine for 20 minutes to rest.
6. Remove from baking pan and put loaf on a cooling rack.

Nutrition Info: Calories: 379, Sodium: 296 mg, Dietary Fiber: 1.0 g, Fat: 13.7 g, Carbs: 61.25 g, Protein: 5.3 g.

Low-carb Multigrain Bread

Servings: 1 Loaf
Cooking Time: 1 Hour And 30 Minutes
Ingredients:
- ¾ cup whole-wheat flour
- ¼ cup cornmeal
- ¼ cup oatmeal
- Two tablespoons 7-grain cereals
- Two tablespoons baking powder
- One teaspoon salt
- ¼ teaspoon baking soda
- ¾ cup of water
- ¼ cup of vegetable oil
- ¼ cup of orange juice
- Three tablespoons aquafaba

Directions:
1. In the bread pan, add the wet ingredients first, then the dry ingredients.
2. Press the "Quick" or "Cake" mode of your bread machine.
3. Wait until all cycles are through.
4. Remove the bread pan from the machine.
5. Let the bread rest for 10 minutes in the pan before taking it out to cool down further.
6. Slice the bread after an hour has passed.

Nutrition Info: Calories: 60;Carbohydrates: 9g;Fat: 2g;Protein: 1g

Slider Buns

Servings: 18
Cooking Time: 3 Hours
Ingredients:
- 1 1/4 cups milk
- 1 egg
- 2 tablespoons butter
- 3/4 teaspoon salt
- 1/4 cup white sugar
- 3 3/4 cups all-purpose flour
- 1 package active dry yeast
- Flour, for surface

Directions:
1. Add all ingredients to the pan of your bread maker in the order listed above.
2. Set bread machine to Dough cycle. Once the Dough cycle is complete, roll dough out on a floured surface to about a 1-inch thickness.
3. Cut out 18 buns with a biscuit cutter or small glass and place them on a greased baking sheet.
4. Let buns rise about one hour or until they have doubled in size.
5. Bake at 350°F for 10 minutes.
6. Brush the tops of baked buns with melted butter and serve.

Nutrition Info: Calories: 130, Sodium: 118 mg, Dietary Fiber: 0.8g, Fat: 2.2 g, Carbs: 23.7 g, Protein: 3.7 g.

50/50 Bread

Servings: 12 Slices
Cooking Time: 15 Minutes
Ingredients:
- 1 Pound loaf
- ½ cup Lukewarm water
- ½ tbspHoney
- 1 tbsp Unsalted butter, diced
- ¾ cup Plain bread flour
- ¾ cup Whole wheat flour
- ¾ tbsp Brown sugar
- ¾ tbsp Powdered milk
- ¾ tsp Salt
- ½ tsp Instant dry yeast

Directions:
1. Preparing the Ingredients
2. Add the ingredients into the bread machine as per the order of the ingredients listed above or follow your bread machine's instruction manual.
3. Select the Bake cycle
4. Select the whole-wheat setting and medium crust function.
5. When ready, turn the bread out onto a drying rack and allow it to cool, then serve.

Buttermilk Honey Bread

Servings: 14 Slices
Cooking Time: 3 H. 35 Min.
Ingredients:
- ½ cup water
- ¾ cup buttermilk
- ¼ cup honey
- 3 Tbsp butter, softened and cut into pieces
- 3 cups bread flour
- 1½ tsp salt
- 2¼ tsp yeast (or 1 package)

Directions:
1. Add each ingredient to the bread machine in the order and at the temperature recommended by your bread machine manufacturer.
2. Close the lid, select the basic bread, medium crust setting on your bread machine and press start.
3. When the bread machine has finished baking, remove the bread and put it on a cooling rack.

Apricot Oat

Servings: 1 Loaf

Cooking Time: 25 Minutes
Ingredients:
- 4 1/4 cups bread flour
- 2/3 cup rolled oats
- One tablespoon white sugar
- Two teaspoons active dry yeast
- 1 1/2 teaspoons salt
- One teaspoon ground cinnamon
- Two tablespoons butter cut up
- 1 2/3 cups orange juice
- 1/2 cup diced dried apricots
- Two tablespoons honey, warmed

Directions:
1. Into the bread machine's pan, put the bread ingredients in the order suggested by the manufacturer. Then pout in dried apricots before the knead cycle completes.
2. Immediately remove bread from a machine when it's done and then glaze with warmed honey. Let to cool thoroughly before serving.

Nutrition Info: Calories: 80 calories;Total Carbohydrate: 14.4 g ;Cholesterol: 5 mg ;Total Fat: 2.3 g ;Protein: 1.3 g ;Sodium: 306 mg

Healthy Bran Bread

Servings: 1 Loaf
Cooking Time: 10 Minutes
Ingredients:
- 12 slice bread (1½ pounds)
- 1⅛ cups milk, at 80°F to 90°F
- 2¼ tablespoons melted butter, cooled
- 1½ tablespoons unsalted butter, melted
- 3 tablespoons sugar
- 1½ teaspoons salt
- ½ cup wheat bran
- 2⅔ cups white bread flour
- 1½ teaspoon bread machine or instant yeast

Directions:
1. Preparing the Ingredients.
2. Measure and add the ingredients to the pan in the order mentioned above. Place the pan in the bread machine and close the lid.
3. Select the Bake cycle
4. Turn on the bread maker. Select the White / Basic or Whole Wheat setting, then select the dough size and crust color. Press start to start the cycle.
5. When this is done, and the bread is baked, remove the pan from the machine. Let stand a few minutes.
6. Remove the bread from the pan and leave it on a wire rack to cool for at least 10 minutes. Slice and serve.

Italian White Bread

Servings: 14 Slices
Cooking Time: 3 H.
Ingredients:
- ¾ cup cold water
- 2 cups bread flour
- 1 Tbsp sugar
- 1 tsp salt
- 1 Tbsp olive oil
- 1 tsp active dry yeast

Directions:
1. Add each ingredient to the bread machine in the order and at the temperature recommended by your bread machine manufacturer.
2. Close the lid, select the Italian or basic bread, low crust setting on your bread machine, and press start.
3. When the bread machine has finished baking, remove the bread and put it on a cooling rack.

All-purpose White Bread

Servings: 1 Loaf
Cooking Time: 40 Minutes
Ingredients:
- ¾ cup water at 80 degrees F
- One tablespoon melted butter cooled
- One tablespoon sugar
- ¾ teaspoon salt
- Two tablespoons skim milk powder
- 2 cups white bread flour
- ¾ teaspoon instant yeast

Directions:
1. Add all of the ingredients to your bread machine, carefully following the instructions of the manufacturer.
2. Set the program of your bread machine to Basic/White Bread and set crust type to Medium.
3. Press START.
4. Wait until the cycle completes.
5. Once the loaf is ready, take the bucket out and let the loaf cool for 5 minutes.
6. Gently shake the bucket to remove the loaf.
7. Put to a cooling rack, slice, and serve.

Nutrition Info: Calories: 140 Cal;Fat: 2 g ;Carbohydrates:27 g ;Protein: 44 g ;Fibre: 2 g

Mom's White Bread

Servings: 16 Slices
Cooking Time: 3 H.
Ingredients:
- 1 cup and 3 Tbsp water
- 2 Tbsp vegetable oil

- 1½ tsp salt
- 2 Tbsp sugar
- 3¼ cups white bread flour
- 2 tsp active dry yeast

Directions:

1. Add each ingredient to the bread machine in the order and at the temperature recommended by your bread machine manufacturer.
2. Close the lid, select the basic or white bread, medium crust setting on your bread machine, and press start.
3. When the bread machine has finished baking, remove the bread and put it on a cooling rack.

Gluten-free White Bread

Servings: 14 Slices
Cooking Time: 3 H.

Ingredients:

- 2 eggs
- 1⅓ cups milk
- 6 Tbsp oil
- 1 tsp vinegar
- 3⅝ cups white bread flour
- 1 tsp salt
- 2 Tbsp sugar
- 2 tsp dove farm quick yeast

Directions:

1. Add each ingredient to the bread machine in the order and at the temperature recommended by your bread machine manufacturer.
2. Close the lid and start the machine on the gluten free bread program, if available. Alternatively use the basic or rapid setting with a dark crust option.
3. When the bread machine has finished baking, remove the bread and put it on a cooling rack.

Easy Gluten-free, Dairy-free Bread

Servings: 12
Cooking Time: 15 Minutes

Ingredients:

- 1 1/2 cups warm water
- 2 teaspoons active dry yeast
- 2 teaspoons sugar
- 2 eggs, room temperature
- 1 egg white, room temperature
- 1 1/2 tablespoons apple cider vinegar
- 4 1/2 tablespoons olive oil
- 3 1/3 cups multi-purpose gluten-free flour

Directions:

1. Preparing the Ingredients

2. Add the yeast and sugar to the warm water and stir to mix in a large mixing bowl; set aside until foamy, about 8 to 10 minutes.
3. Whisk the 2 eggs and 1 egg white together in a separate mixing bowl and add to baking pan of bread maker.
4. Add apple cider vinegar and oil to baking pan.
5. Add foamy yeast/water mixture to baking pan.
6. Add the multi-purpose gluten-free flour on top.
7. Select the Bake cycle
8. Set for Gluten-Free bread setting and Start.
9. Remove and invert pan onto a cooling rack to remove the bread from the baking pan. Allow to cool completely before slicing to serve.

Autumn Treasures Loaf

Servings: 1 Loaf
Cooking Time: 1 Hour And 30 Minutes
Ingredients:
- 1 cup all-purpose flour
- ½ cup dried fruit, chopped
- ¼ cup pecans, chopped
- ¼ cup of sugar
- Two tablespoons baking powder
- One teaspoon salt
- ¼ teaspoon of baking soda
- ½ teaspoon ground nutmeg
- 1 cup apple juice
- ¼ cup of vegetable oil
- Three tablespoons aquafaba
- One teaspoon of vanilla extract

Directions:
1. Add all wet ingredients first to the bread pan before the dry ingredients.
2. Turn on the bread machine with the "Quick" or "Cake" setting.
3. Wait for all cycles to be finished.
4. Remove the bread pan from the machine.
5. After 10 minutes, transfer the bread from the pan into a wire rack.
6. Slice the bread only when it has completely cooled down.

Nutrition Info: Calories: 80;Carbohydrates: 12g;Fat: 3g;Protein: 1g

Crusty French Bread

Servings: 1 Loaf
Cooking Time: 10 Minutes
Ingredients:
- 12 slice bread (1½ pound)
- 1 cup water, at 80°F to 90°F
- 1¼ tablespoons olive oil
- 2 tablespoons sugar

- 1¼ teaspoons salt
- 3 cups white bread flour
- 1¼ teaspoons bread machine or instant yeast, or flax seeds (optional)

Directions:
1. Preparing the Ingredients.
2. Place the ingredients in your bread machine as recommended by the manufacturer.
3. Select the Bake cycle
4. Program the machine for French bread, select light or medium crust, and press Start.
5. When this is done, and the bread is baked, remove the pan from the machine. Let stand a few minutes.
6. Remove the bread from the pan and leave it on a wire rack to cool for at least 10 minutes.

Warm Spiced Pumpkin Bread

Servings: One Loaf (12 Slices)
Cooking Time: 60 To 75 Minutes
Ingredients:
- 1½ cups pumpkin purée
- Three eggs, at room temperature
- 1/3 cup melted butter cooled
- 1 cup of sugar
- 3 cups all-purpose flour
- 1½ teaspoons baking powder
- ¾ teaspoon ground cinnamon
- ½ teaspoon baking soda
- ¼ teaspoon ground nutmeg
- ¼ teaspoon ground ginger
- ¼ teaspoon salt
- Pinch ground cloves

Directions:
1. Lightly grease the bread bucket with butter.
2. Add the pumpkin, eggs, butter, and sugar.
3. Program the machine for Quick/Rapid setting and press Start.
4. Let the wet ingredients be mixed by the paddles until the first fast mixing cycle is finished, about 10 minutes into the process.
5. While the wet ingredients are mixing
6. stir together the flour, baking powder, cinnamon, baking soda, nutmeg
7. ginger, salt, and cloves until well blended.
8. Add the dry ingredients to the bucket when the second fast mixing cycle starts.
9. Scrape down the sides of the bucket once after the dry ingredients are mixed into the wet.
10. When the loaf is finished, remove the bucket from the machine.
11. Let it cool for five minutes.
12. Gently shake the bucket to remove the bread and turn it out onto a rack to cool.

Nutrition Info: Calories: 251;Fat: 7g ;Carbohydrates: 43g;Fibre: 2g;Sodium: 159mg;Protein: 5g

Double-chocolate Zucchini Bread

Servings: 1 Loaf
Cooking Time: 10 Minutes
Ingredients:
- 225 grams grated zucchini
- 125 grams All-Purpose Flour Blend
- 50 grams all-natural unsweetened cocoa powder (not Dutch-process)
- 1 teaspoon xanthan gum
- ¾ teaspoon baking soda
- ¼ teaspoon baking powder
- ¼ teaspoon salt
- ½ teaspoon ground espresso
- 135 grams chocolate chips or nondairy alternative
- 100 grams cane sugar or granulated sugar
- 2 large eggs
- ¼ cup avocado oil or canola oil
- 60 grams vanilla Greek yogurt or nondairy alternative
- 1 teaspoon vanilla extract

Directions:
1. Preparing the Ingredients.
2. Measure and add the ingredients to the pan in the order mentioned above. Place the pan in the bread machine and close the lid.
3. Select the Bake cycle
4. Turn on the bread maker. Select the White / Basic setting, then select the dough size, select light or medium crust. Press start to start the cycle.
5. When this is done, and the bread is baked, remove the pan from the machine. Let stand a few minutes.
6. Remove the bread from the skillet and leave it on a wire rack to cool for at least 15 minutes. Store leftovers in an airtight container at room temperature for up to 5 days, or freeze to enjoy a slice whenever you desire. Let each slice thaw naturally

SOURDOUGH BREAD

Basic Sourdough Bread

Servings: 1 Loaf
Cooking Time: 10 Minutes
Ingredients:
- 12 slice bread (1½ pounds)
- 2 cups Simple Sourdough Starter (here), fed, active, and at room temperature
- 2 tablespoons water, at 80°F to 90°F
- ¾ teaspoon apple cider vinegar
- 1⅓ teaspoons sugar
- 1 teaspoon salt
- 1⅔ cups white bread flour
- ½ cup nonfat dry milk powder
- 1 teaspoon bread machine or instant yeast

Directions:
1. Preparing the Ingredients.
2. Choose the size of loaf of your preference and then measure the ingredients.
3. Add all of the ingredients mentioned previously in the list, close the lid after placing the pan in the bread machine.
4. Select the Bake cycle
5. Turn on the bread machine. Select the White/Basic setting, select the loaf size, and the crust color. Press start.
6. When the cycle is finished, carefully remove the pan from the bread maker and let rest. When the machine signals to add ingredients, add the chopped pecans.
7. Remove the bread from the pan, put in a wire rack to cool for at least 5 minutes, and slice.

Faux Sourdough Bread

Servings: 1 Loaf
Cooking Time: 10 Minutes
Ingredients:
- 12 slice bread (1½ pounds)
- ¾ cup plus 1 tablespoon water, at 80°F to 90°F
- ⅓ cup sour cream, at room temperature
- 2¼ tablespoons melted butter, cooled
- 1½ tablespoons apple cider vinegar
- ¾ tablespoon sugar
- ¾ teaspoon salt
- 3 cups white bread flour
- 1 teaspoon bread machine or instant yeast

Directions:
1. Preparing the Ingredients.
2. Choose the size of loaf of your preference and then measure the ingredients.
3. Add all of the ingredients mentioned previously in the list, close the lid after placing the pan in the bread machine.
4. Select the Bake cycle

5. Turn on the bread machine. Select the Wheat/Whole-Grain bread setting, select the loaf size, select medium crust color. Press start.
6. When the cycle is finished, carefully remove the pan from the bread maker and let it rest.
7. Remove the bread from the pan, put in a wire rack to cool for at least 10 minutes, and slice.

Cheese Potato Bread

Servings: 1 Loaf
Cooking Time: 10 Minutes
Ingredients:
- 12 slice bread (1½ pounds)
- 1 cup lukewarm water
- 2¼ tablespoons vegetable oil
- 2 large eggs, beaten
- ⅓ cup dry skim milk powder
- 3 tablespoons sugar
- ¾ teaspoon apple cider vinegar
- 1⅛ teaspoons table salt
- ⅓ cup cornstarch
- ½ cup cottage cheese
- 3 tablespoons snipped chives
- ⅓ cup instant potato buds
- ⅓ cup potato starch
- ⅓ cup tapioca flour
- 1½ cups white rice flour
- 1½ teaspoons bread machine yeast

Directions:
1. Preparing the Ingredients.
2. Choose the size of loaf of your preference and then measure the ingredients.
3. Add all of the ingredients mentioned previously in the list, close the lid after placing the pan in the bread machine.
4. Select the Bake cycle
5. Turn on the bread machine. Select the White/ Basic or Gluten-Free (if your machine has this setting) setting, select the loaf size, and the crust color. Press start.
6. When the cycle is finished, carefully remove the pan from the bread maker and let it rest.
7. Remove the bread from the pan, put in a wire rack to cool for at least 10 minutes, and slice.

Instant Cocoa Bread

Servings: 1 Loaf
Cooking Time: 10 Minutes
Ingredients:
- 12 slice bread (1½ pounds)
- 1⅛ cups lukewarm water
- 2 large eggs, beaten
- 2¼ tablespoons molasses
- 1½ tablespoons canola oil

- ¾ teaspoon apple cider vinegar
- 2¼ tablespoons light brown sugar
- 1⅛ teaspoons table salt
- 1½ cups white rice flour
- ½ cup potato starch
- ¼ cup tapioca flour
- 1½ teaspoons xanthan gum
- 1½ teaspoons cocoa powder
- 1½ teaspoons instant coffee granules
- 2 teaspoons bread machine yeast

Directions:
1. Preparing the Ingredients.
2. Choose the size of loaf of your preference and then measure the ingredients.
3. Add all of the ingredients mentioned previously in the list, close the lid after placing the pan in the bread machine Select the Bake cycle
4. Turn on the bread machine. Select the White/Basic or Gluten-Free (if your machine has this setting) setting, select the loaf size, select light or medium crust. Press start.
5. When the cycle is finished, carefully remove the pan from the bread maker and let it rest.
6. Remove the bread from the pan, put in a wire rack to cool for at least 10 minutes, and slice.

San Francisco Sourdough Bread

Servings: 1 Loaf
Cooking Time: 10 Minutes
Ingredients:
- 12 slice bread (1½ pounds)
- 1 cup plus 2 tablespoons Simple Sourdough Starter (here) or No-Yeast Sourdough Starter (here), fed, active, and at room temperature
- ½ cup plus 1 tablespoon water, at 80°F to 90°F
- 2¼ tablespoons olive oil
- 1½ teaspoons salt
- 2 tablespoons sugar
- 1½ tablespoons skim milk powder
- ⅓ cup whole-wheat flour
- 2⅔ cups white bread flour
- 1⅔ teaspoons bread machine or instant yeast

Directions:
1. Preparing the Ingredients.
2. Choose the size of loaf of your preference and then measure the ingredients.
3. Add all of the ingredients mentioned previously in the list, close the lid after placing the pan in the bread machine
4. Select the Bake cycle
5. Turn on the bread machine. Select the White/Basic setting, select the loaf size, and the crust color. Press start.
6. When the cycle is finished, carefully remove the pan from the bread maker and let it rest.
7. Remove the bread from the pan, put in a wire rack to cool for at least 10 minutes, and slice.

Sourdough Cheddar Bread

Servings: 1 Loaf
Cooking Time: 10 Minutes
Ingredients:
- 12 slice bread (1½ pounds)
- 1 cup Simple Sourdough Starter or No-Yeast Sourdough Starter, fed, active, and at room temperature
- ⅓ cup water, at 80°F to 90°F
- 4 teaspoons sugar
- 1 teaspoon salt
- ½ cup (2 ounces) grated aged Cheddar cheese
- ⅔ cup whole-wheat flour
- ¼ cup oat bran
- 1⅓ cups white bread flour
- 1½ teaspoons bread machine or instant yeast

Directions:
1. Preparing the Ingredients.
2. Choose the size of loaf of your preference and then measure the ingredients.
3. Add all of the ingredients mentioned previously in the list, close the lid after placing the pan in the bread machine
4. Select the Bake cycle
5. Turn on the bread machine. Select the Wheat/Whole-Grain bread setting, select the loaf size, and the crust color. Press start. When the cycle is finished, carefully remove the pan from the bread maker and let it rest.
6. Remove the bread from the pan, put in a wire rack to cool for at least 5 minutes, and slice.

Pecan Cranberry Bread

Servings: 1 Loaf
Cooking Time: 10 Minutes
Ingredients:
- 12 slice bread (1½ pounds)
- 1⅛ cups lukewarm water
- 3 tablespoons canola oil
- ¾ tablespoon orange zest
- ¾ teaspoon apple cider vinegar
- 2 eggs, slightly beaten
- 2¼ tablespoons sugar
- ¾ teaspoon table salt
- 1½ cups white rice flour
- ½ cup nonfat dry milk powder
- ⅓ cup tapioca flour
- ⅓ cup potato starch
- ¼ cup corn starch
- ¾ tablespoon xanthan gum
- 1½ teaspoons bread machine yeast
- ½ cup dried cranberries

- ½ cup pecan pieces

Directions:
1. Preparing the Ingredients.
2. Choose the size of loaf of your preference and then measure the ingredients.
3. Add all of the ingredients mentioned previously in the list, close the lid after placing the pan in the bread machine. Select the Bake cycle
4. Turn on the bread maker. Select the Gluten Free or Fruit/Nut (if your machine has this setting) setting, then the loaf size, and finally the crust color. Start the cycle. (If you don't have either of the above settings, use Basic/White.).
5. When the machine signals to add ingredients, add the pecans and cranberries. (Some machines have a fruit/nut hopper where you can add the pecans and cranberries when you start the machine. The machine will automatically add them to the dough during the baking process.).
6. When the cycle is finished, carefully remove the pan from the bread maker and let it rest.
7. Remove the bread from the pan, put in a wire rack to cool for at least 10 minutes, and slice.

Lemon Sourdough Bread

Servings: 1 Loaf
Cooking Time: 10 Minutes
Ingredients:
- 12 slice bread (1½ pounds)
- ¾ cup Simple Sourdough Starter (here) or No-Yeast Sourdough Starter (here), fed, active, and at room temperature
- ¾ cup water, at 80°F to 90°F
- 1 egg, at room temperature
- 3 tablespoons butter, melted and cooled
- ⅓ cup honey
- 1½ teaspoons salt
- 2 teaspoons lemon zest
- 1½ teaspoons lime zest
- ⅓ cup wheat germ
- 3 cups white bread flour
- 1¾ teaspoons bread machine or instant yeast

Directions:
1. Preparing the Ingredients.
2. Choose the size of loaf of your preference and then measure the ingredients.
3. Add all of the ingredients mentioned previously in the list, close the lid after placing the pan in the bread machine Select the Bake cycle.
4. Turn on the bread machine. Select the Whole-Wheat/Whole-Grain bread setting, select the loaf size, select light or medium crust. Press start.
5. When the cycle is finished, carefully remove the pan from the bread maker and let it rest.
6. Remove the bread from the pan, put in a wire rack to cool for at least 10 minutes, and slice.

No-yeast Whole-wheat Sourdough Starter

Servings: 2 Cups (32 Servings)
Cooking Time: 10 Minutes Plus Fermenting Time

Ingredients:
- 1 cup whole-wheat flour, divided
- ½ teaspoon honey
- 1 cup chlorine-free bottled water, at room temperature, divided

Directions:
1. Preparing the Ingredients.
2. Stir together ½ cup of flour, ½ cup of water, and the honey in a large glass bowl with a wooden spoon. Loosely cover the bowl with plastic wrap and place it in a warm area for 5 days, stirring at least twice a day. After 5 days, stir in the remaining ½ cup of flour and ½ cup of water.
3. Select the Bake cycle
4. Cover the bowl loosely again with plastic wrap and place it in a warm area.
5. When the starter has bubbles and foam on top, it is ready to use.
6. Store the starter in the refrigerator in a covered glass jar, and stir it before using. If you use half, replenish the starter with ½ cup flour and ½ cup water

Classic White Bread

Servings: 1 Loaf
Cooking Time: 10 Minutes

Ingredients:
- 12 slice bread (1½ pounds)
- 1¼ cup lukewarm water
- 3 tablespoons canola oil
- ¾ teaspoon apple cider vinegar
- 2 eggs, room temperature, slightly beaten
- 1½ cups white rice flour
- ⅔ cup tapioca flour
- ½ cup nonfat dry milk powder
- ½ cup potato starch
- ⅓ cup cornstarch
- 2 tablespoon sugar
- ⅔ tablespoon xanthan gum
- ⅔ teaspoon table salt
- 1¼ teaspoons bread machine yeast

Directions:
1. Preparing the Ingredients.
2. Choose the size of loaf of your preference and then measure the ingredients.
3. Add all of the ingredients mentioned previously in the list, close the lid after placing the pan in the bread machine.
4. Select the Bake cycle
5. Turn on the bread machine. Select the White/Basic setting, select the loaf size, and the crust color. Press start.
6. When the cycle is finished, carefully remove the pan from the bread maker and let it rest.
7. Remove the bread from the pan, put in a wire rack to cool for at least 10 minutes, and slice.

Pecan Apple Spice Bread

Servings: 1 Loaf
Cooking Time: 10 Minutes
Ingredients:
- 12 slice bread (1½ pounds)
- ⅓ cup lukewarm water
- 2¼ tablespoons canola oil
- ¾ teaspoon apple cider vinegar
- 2¼ tablespoons light brown sugar, packed
- ¾ cup Granny Smith apples, grated
- 2 eggs, room temperature, slightly beaten
- ½ cup nonfat dry milk powder
- ½ cup brown rice flour
- ½ cup tapioca flour
- ½ cup millet flour
- ⅓ cup corn starch
- 1½ tablespoons apple pie spice
- ¾ tablespoon xanthan gum
- ¾ teaspoon table salt
- 1¼ teaspoons bread machine yeast
- ⅓ cup pecans, chopped

Directions:
1.   Preparing the Ingredients.
2.   Choose the size of loaf of your preference and then measure the ingredients.
3.   Add all of the ingredients mentioned previously in the list, close the lid after placing the pan in the bread machine.
4.   Select the Bake cycle
5.   Turn on the bread machine. Select the White/Basic setting, select the loaf size, and the crust color. Press start.
6.   When the cycle is finished, carefully remove the pan from the bread maker and let rest. When the machine signals to add ingredients, add the chopped pecans.
7.   Remove the bread from the pan, put in a wire rack to cool for at least 10 minutes, and slice.

Dark Chocolate Sourdough

Servings: 1 Loaf
Cooking Time: 10 Minutes
Ingredients:
- 12 slice bread (1½ pounds)
- 2 cups No-Yeast Sourdough Starter, fed, active, and at room temperature
- 2 tablespoons water, at 80°F to 90°F
- 2 tablespoons melted butter, cooled
- ¾ teaspoon pure vanilla extract
- 2 teaspoons sugar
- 1½ teaspoons salt
- ⅓ teaspoon ground cinnamon
- ¼ cup unsweetened cocoa powder

- 2½ cups white bread flour
- 1½ teaspoons bread machine or instant yeast
- ½ cup semisweet chocolate chips
- ⅓ cup chopped pistachios
- ⅓ cup raisins

Directions:
1. Preparing the Ingredients.
2. Choose the size of loaf of your preference and then measure the ingredients.
3. Add all of the ingredients mentioned previously in the list, close the lid after placing the pan in the bread machine
4. Select the Bake cycle
5. Turn on the bread machine. Select the Wheat/Whole-Grain bread setting, select the loaf size, and the crust color. Press start. When the cycle is finished, carefully remove the pan from the bread maker and let it rest.
6. Remove the bread from the pan, put in a wire rack to cool for at least 5 minutes, and slice

Sourdough Beer Bread

Servings: 1 Loaf
Cooking Time: 10 Minutes
Ingredients:
- 12 slice bread (1½ pounds)
- 1 cup Simple Sourdough Starter (here) or No-Yeast Sourdough Starter (here), fed, active, and at room temperature
- ½ cup plus 1 tablespoon dark beer, at 80°F to 90°F
- 1½ tablespoons melted butter, cooled
- ¾ tablespoon sugar
- 1⅛ teaspoons salt
- 2⅔ cups white bread flour
- 1⅛ teaspoons bread machine or instant yeast

Directions:
1. Preparing the Ingredients.
2. Choose the size of loaf of your preference and then measure the ingredients.
3. Add all of the ingredients mentioned previously in the list, close the lid after placing the pan in the bread machine
4. Select the Bake cycle
5. Turn on the bread machine. Select the Wheat/Whole-Grain bread setting, select the loaf size, and the crust color. Press start.
6. When the cycle is finished, carefully remove the pan from the bread maker and let it rest.
7. Remove the bread from the pan, put in a wire rack to cool for at least 10 minutes, and slice.

Sourdough Milk Bread

Servings: 1 Loaf
Cooking Time: 10 Minutes
Ingredients:
- 12 slice bread (1½ pounds)

- 1½ cups Simple Sourdough Starter (here) or No-Yeast Sourdough Starter (here), fed, active, and at room temperature
- ⅓ cup milk, at 80°F to 90°F
- 3 tablespoons olive oil
- 1½ tablespoons honey
- 1 teaspoon salt
- 3 cups white bread flour
- 1 teaspoon bread machine or instant yeast

Directions:
1. Preparing the Ingredients.
2. Choose the size of loaf of your preference and then measure the ingredients.
3. Add all of the ingredients mentioned previously in the list, close the lid after placing the pan in the bread machine.
4. Select the Bake cycle
5. Turn on the bread machine. Select the White/Basic setting, select the loaf size, and the crust color. Press start.
6. When the cycle is finished, carefully remove the pan from the bread maker and let it rest.
7. Remove the bread from the pan, put in a wire rack to cool for at least 10 minutes, and slice.

SPECIALTY BREAD

French Butter Bread

Servings: 1 Loaf

Ingredients:
- 16 slice bread (2 pounds)
- ¾ cup lukewarm milk
- 4 eggs, at room temperature
- 2⅔ tablespoons sugar
- 1 teaspoon table salt
- ½ cup + 3⅓ tablespoons unsalted butter, melted
- 4 cups white bread flour
- 2 teaspoons bread machine yeast
- 12 slice bread (1½ pounds)
- ½ cup + 1 tablespoon lukewarm milk
- 3 eggs, at room temperature
- 2 tablespoons sugar
- ¾ teaspoon table salt
- ½ cup unsalted butter, melted
- 3 cups white bread flour
- 1½ teaspoons bread machine yeast

Directions:
1. Choose the size of loaf you would like to make and measure your ingredients.
2. Add the ingredients to the bread pan in the order listed above.
3. Place the pan in the bread machine and close the lid.
4. Turn on the bread maker. Select the White/Basic setting, then the loaf size, and finally the crust color. Start the cycle.
5. When the cycle is finished and the bread is baked, carefully remove the pan from the machine. Use a potholder as the handle will be very hot. Let rest for a few minutes.
6. Remove the bread from the pan and allow to cool on a wire rack for at least 10 minutes before slicing.

Nutrition Info: (Per Serving):Calories 208, fat 8.8 g, carbs 24.3 g, sodium 221 mg, protein 5.8 g

Raisin Keto Bread

Servings: 15

Cooking Time: 3 Hours And 25 Minutes

Ingredients:
- Coconut flour – ½ cup
- Almond flour – ½ cup
- Psyllium husk powder - 6 tbsp.
- Chopped raisins – ¼ cup
- Swerve – 2 tbsp.
- Baking powder – 1 tbsp.
- Ground cinnamon – ½ tsp.
- Salt, to taste – ¼ tsp.
- Egg whites - 2 cups

- Butter – 3 tbsp., melted
- Apple cider vinegar – 2 tbsp.

Directions:
1. Add everything in the bread machine in the order recommended by the machine manufacturer.
2. Select Basic bread setting and choose crust. Press Start.
3. Remove the bread when done.
4. Cool, slice, and serve.

Nutrition Info: (Per Serving): Calories: 120; Total Fat: 4 g; Saturated Fat: 2.3 g; Carbohydrates: 9 g; Cholesterol: 6 mg; Fiber: 11.1 g; Calcium: 48 mg; Sodium: 89 mg; Protein: 5.4 g

New Year Spiced Bread

Servings: 1 Loaf

Ingredients:
- 16 slice bread (2 pounds)
- ½ cup brewed coffee, cooled to room temperature
- ⅔ cup unsalted butter, melted
- ⅔ cup honey
- 1 cup sugar
- ⅓ cup dark brown sugar
- 2 eggs, at room temperature
- 3 tablespoons whiskey
- ⅓ cup orange juice, at room temperature
- 1⅓ teaspoons pure vanilla extract
- 3 cups all-purpose flour
- ⅔ tablespoon ground cinnamon
- ⅔ teaspoon baking soda
- ⅓ teaspoon ground allspice
- ⅓ teaspoon table salt
- ⅓ teaspoon ground cloves
- ⅔ tablespoon baking powder
- 12 slice bread (1½ pounds)
- ⅓ cup brewed coffee, cooled to room temperature
- ½ cup unsalted butter, melted
- ½ cup honey
- ¾ cup sugar
- ¼ cup dark brown sugar
- 2 eggs, at room temperature
- 2 tablespoons whiskey
- ¼ cup orange juice, at room temperature
- 1 teaspoon pure vanilla extract
- 2 cups all-purpose flour
- ½ tablespoon ground cinnamon
- ½ teaspoon baking soda
- ¼ teaspoon ground allspice
- ¼ teaspoon table salt

- ¼ teaspoon ground cloves
- ½ tablespoon baking powder

Directions:
1. Choose the size of loaf you would like to make and measure your ingredients.
2. Add the ingredients to the bread pan in the order listed above.
3. Place the pan in the bread machine and close the lid.
4. Turn on the bread maker. Select the Quick/Rapid setting, then the loaf size, and finally the crust color. Start the cycle.
5. When the cycle is finished and the bread is baked, carefully remove the pan from the machine. Use a potholder as the handle will be very hot. Let rest for a few minutes.
6. Remove the bread from the pan and allow to cool on a wire rack for at least 10 minutes before slicing.

Nutrition Info: (Per Serving):Calories 271, fat 8.7 g, carbs 38.3 g, sodium 168 mg, protein 3.4 g

FRUIT AND VEGETABLE BREAD

Lemon-lime Blueberry Bread

Servings: 1 Loaf
Cooking Time: 10 Minutes
Ingredients:
- 12 slice bread (1½ pounds)
- ¾ cup plain yogurt, at room temperature
- ½ cup water, at 80°F to 90°F
- 3 tablespoons honey
- 1 tablespoon melted butter, cooled
- 1½ teaspoons salt
- ½ teaspoon lemon extract
- 1 teaspoon lime zest
- 1 cup dried blueberries
- 3 cups white bread flour
- 2¼ teaspoons bread machine or instant yeast

Directions:
1. Preparing the Ingredients.
2. Choose the size of loaf of your preference and then measure the ingredients.
3. Add all of the ingredients mentioned previously in the list. Close the lid after placing the pan in the bread machine
4. Select the Bake cycle
5. Turn on the bread machine. Select the White/Basic setting, select the loaf size, and the crust color. Press start.
6. When the cycle is finished, carefully remove the pan from the bread maker and let it rest.
7. Remove the bread from the pan, put in a wire rack to cool. Cool completely, about 10 minutes. Slice

Caramelized Onion Focaccia Bread

Servings: 4
Cooking Time: 10 Minutes
Ingredients:
- 3/4 cup water
- 2 tablespoons olive oil
- 1 tablespoon sugar
- 1 teaspoon salt
- 2 cups flour
- 1 1/2 teaspoons yeast
- 3/4 cup mozzarella cheese, shredded
- 2 tablespoons parmesan cheese, shredded
- Onion topping:
- 3 tablespoons butter
- 2 medium onions
- 2 cloves garlic, minced

Directions:

1.   Preparing the Ingredients
2.   Place all ingredients, except cheese and onion topping, in your bread maker in the order listed above. Grease a large baking sheet. Pat dough into a 12-inch circle on the pan; cover and let rise in warm place for about 30 minutes.
3.   Melt butter in large frying pan over medium-low heat. Cook onions and garlic in butter 15 minutes, stirring often, until onions are caramelized.
4.   Preheat an oven to 400°F.
5.   Make deep depressions across the dough at 1-inch intervals with the handle of a wooden spoon. Spread the onion topping over dough and sprinkle with cheeses.
6.   Bake 15 to 20 minutes or until golden brown. Cut into wedges and serve warm.

Perfect Sweet Potato Bread

Servings: 10
Cooking Time: 3 Hours
Ingredients:
- Sweet potato – 1, mashed
- Milk powder – 2 tbsps.
- Salt – 1 ½ tsps.
- Brown sugar – 1/3 cup.
- Butter – 2 tbsps., softened
- Cinnamon – ½ tsp.
- Bread flour – 4 cups.
- Vanilla extract – 1 tsp.
- Warm water – ½ cup.

Directions:
1.   Add water, vanilla, bread flour, cinnamon, butter, brown sugar, salt, yeast, milk powder, and sweet potato into the bread machine pan. Select white bread setting then select light crust and press start. Once loaf is done, remove the loaf pan from the machine. Allow it to cool for 10 minutes. Slice and serve.

Olive Rosemary Bread

Servings: 10
Cooking Time: 3 Hours 27 Minutes
Ingredients:
- Water – 1 cup.
- Olives – 1 cup., pitted and quartered
- Salt – 1 tsp.
- Sugar – 1 tbsp.
- Olive oil – 2 tbsps.
- Bread flour – 3 ¼ cups.
- Rosemary – ¼ cup., chopped
- Instant yeast – 1 ¼ tsp.

Directions:

1. Add all ingredients into the bread machine pan. Select sweet bread setting then select medium crust and start. Once loaf is done, remove the loaf pan from the machine. Allow it to cool for 10 minutes. Slice and serve.

Sweet Potato Bread

Servings: 1 Loaf
Cooking Time: 10 Minutes
Ingredients:
- 12 slice bread (1½ pounds)
- ⅓ cup + 2 tablespoons lukewarm water
- ¾ cup plain sweet potatoes, peeled and mashed
- 1½ tablespoons unsalted butter, melted
- ¼ cup dark brown sugar
- 1 teaspoon table salt
- 3 cups bread flour
- ⅛ teaspoon ground nutmeg
- ⅛ teaspoon cinnamon
- ¾ teaspoon vanilla extract
- 1½ tablespoons dry milk powder
- 1½ teaspoons bread machine yeast

Directions:
1. Preparing the Ingredients.
2. Choose the size of loaf of your preference and then measure the ingredients.
3. Add all of the ingredients mentioned previously in the list.
4. Close the lid after placing the pan in the bread machine.
5. Select the Bake cycle
6. Turn on the bread machine. Select the Quick/Rapid setting, select the loaf size, and the crust color. Press start.
7. When the cycle is finished, carefully remove the pan from the bread maker and let it rest.
8. Remove the bread from the pan, put in a wire rack to Cool about 5 minutes. Slice

Fresh Blueberry Bread

Servings: 1 Loaf
Cooking Time: 10 Minutes
Ingredients:
- 12 to 16 slices (1½ to 2 pounds)
- 1 cup plain Greek yogurt, at room temperature
- ½ cup milk, at room temperature
- 3 tablespoons butter, at room temperature
- 2 eggs, at room temperature
- ½ cup sugar
- ¼ cup light brown sugar
- 1 teaspoon pure vanilla extract
- ½ teaspoon lemon zest
- 2 cups all-purpose flour

- 1 tablespoon baking powder
- ¾ teaspoon salt
- ¼ teaspoon ground nutmeg
- 1 cup blueberries

Directions:
1. Preparing the Ingredients.
2. Place the yogurt, milk, butter, eggs, sugar, brown sugar, vanilla, and zest in your bread machine.
3. Select the Bake cycle.
4. Program the machine for Quick/Rapid bread and press Start. While the wet ingredients are mixing, stir together the flour, baking powder, salt, and nutmeg in a medium bowl. After the first fast mixing is done and the machine signals, add the dry ingredients. When the second mixing cycle is complete, stir in the blueberries. When the loaf is done, remove the bucket from the machine. Let the loaf cool for 5 minutes. Gently shake the bucket to remove the loaf, and turn it out onto a rack to cool.

Monkey Bread

Servings: 12 - 15
Cooking Time: 2 Hours
Ingredients:
- 1 cup water
- 1 cup butter, unsalted
- 2 tablespoons butter, softened
- 3 cups all-purpose flour
- 1 teaspoon ground cinnamon
- 1 teaspoon salt
- 1/4 cup white sugar
- 2 1/2 teaspoons active dry yeast
- 1 cup brown sugar, packed
- 1 cup raisins
- Flour, for surface

Directions:
1. Add ingredients, except 1 cup butter, brown sugar, raisins and yeast, to bread maker pan in order listed above.
2. Make a well in the center of the dry ingredients and add the yeast. Make sure that no liquid comes in contact with the yeast.
3. Select Dough cycle and press Start.
4. Place finished dough on floured surface and knead 10 times.
5. Melt one cup of butter in small saucepan.
6. Stir in brown sugar and raisins and mix until smooth. Remove from heat.
7. Cut dough into one inch chunks.
8. Drop one chunk at a time into the butter sugar mixture. Thoroughly coat dough pieces, then layer them loosely in a greased Bundt pan.
9. Let rise in a warm, draft-free space; about 15 to 20 minutes.
10. Bake at 375°F for 20 to 25 minutes or until golden brown.
11. Remove from oven, plate, and serve warm.

Nutrition Info: Calories: 294, Sodium: 265. Mg, Dietary Fiber: 1.3 g, Fat: 14.1 g, Carbs: 40 g, Protein: 3.3 g.

Brown Bread With Raisins

Servings: 1 Loaf
Cooking Time: 10 Minutes
Ingredients:
- 32 slices
- 1 cup all-purpose flour
- 1 cup whole wheat flour
- 1 cup whole-grain cornmeal
- 1 cup raisins
- 2 cups buttermilk
- ¾ cup molasses
- 2 teaspoons baking soda
- 1 teaspoon salt

Directions:
1. Preparing the Ingredients.
2. Choose the size of loaf of your preference and then measure the ingredients.
3. Add all of the ingredients mentioned previously in the list. Close the lid after placing the pan in the bread machine.
4. Select the Bake cycle
5. Turn on the bread machine. Select the White/Basic setting, select the loaf size, and the crust color. Press start.
6. When the cycle is finished, carefully remove the pan from the bread maker and let it rest.
7. Remove the bread from the pan, put in a wire rack to Cool completely, about 30 minutes.

Sauerkraut Rye Bread

Servings: 1 Loaf
Cooking Time: 10 Minutes
Ingredients:
- 12 slice bread (1½ pounds)
- 1 cup water, at 80°F to 90°F
- 1½ tablespoons melted butter, cooled
- ⅓ cup molasses
- ½ cup drained sauerkraut
- ⅓ teaspoon salt
- 1½ tablespoons unsweetened cocoa powder
- Pinch ground nutmeg
- ¾ cup rye flour
- 2 cups white bread flour
- 1⅔ teaspoons bread machine or instant yeast

Directions:
1. Preparing the Ingredients.
2. Choose the size of loaf of your preference and then measure the ingredients.

3. Add all of the ingredients mentioned previously in the list.
4. Close the lid after placing the pan in the bread machine.
5. Select the Bake cycle
6. Turn on the bread machine. Select the White/Basic setting, select the loaf size, and the crust color. Press start.
7. When the cycle is finished, carefully remove the pan from the bread maker and let it rest.
8. Remove the bread from the pan, put in a wire rack to Cool about 5 minutes. Slice

Gluten-free Glazed Lemon-pecan Bread

Servings: 1 Loaf
Cooking Time: 10 Minutes
Ingredients:
- 12 slice bread (1½ pounds)
- ½ cup white rice flour
- ½ cup tapioca flour
- ½ cup potato starch
- ¼ cup sweet white sorghum flour
- ¼ cup garbanzo and fava flour
- 1 teaspoon xanthan gum
- 1 teaspoon gluten-free baking powder
- 1 teaspoon baking soda
- ½ teaspoon salt
- 2 eggs
- ½ cup sunflower or canola oil or melted ghee
- ¼ cup almond milk, soymilk or regular milk
- ½ teaspoon cider vinegar
- 1 tablespoon grated lemon peel
- ¼ cup fresh lemon juice
- 2/3 cup granulated sugar
- ½ cup chopped pecans
- glaze
- 2 tablespoons fresh lemon juice
- 1 cup gluten-free powdered sugar

Directions:
1. Preparing the Ingredients.
2. Choose the size of loaf of your preference and then measure the ingredients.
3. Add all of the ingredients mentioned previously in the list. Close the lid after placing the pan in the bread machine.
4. Select the Bake cycle.
5. Turn on the bread machine. Select the White/Basic setting, select the loaf size, and the crust color. Press start. When the cycle is finished, carefully remove the pan from the bread maker and let it rest.
6. Remove the bread from the pan, put in a wire rack to Cool about 10 minutes.
7. In small bowl, stir all glaze ingredients until smooth. With fork, poke holes in top of loaf; drizzle glaze over loaf. Serve warm.

Fruit Raisin Bread

Servings: 14 Slices
Cooking Time: 3 H. 5 Min.

Ingredients:
- 1 egg
- 1 cup water plus 2 Tbsp
- ½ tsp ground cardamom.
- 1 tsp salt
- 1½ Tbsp sugar
- ¼ cup butter, softened
- 3 cups bread flour
- 1 tsp bread machine yeast
- ⅓ cup raisins
- ⅓ cup mixed candied fruit

Directions:
1. Add each ingredient except the raisins and fruitcake mix to the bread machine in the order and at the temperature recommended by your bread machine manufacturer.
2. Close the lid, select the basic bread, medium crust setting on your bread machine, and press start.
3. Add raisins and fruit at the fruit/nut beep or 5 to 10 minutes before the last kneading cycle ends.
4. When the bread machine has finished baking, remove the bread and put it on a cooling rack.

Mushroom Leek Bread

Servings: 10
Cooking Time: 2 Hours

Ingredients:
- Butter – 2 tbsps.
- Mushrooms – 2 cups., sliced
- Leeks – ¾ cup., sliced
- Dried thyme – 1 ½ tsps.
- Water – 1 1/3 cup.
- Salt – 1 ½ tsps.
- Honey – 2 tbsps.
- Whole wheat flour – 1 ¼ cups.
- Bread flour – 3 cups.
- Yeast – 1 tsp.

Directions:
1. Heat butter into the saucepan over medium-high heat. Add leeks, mushrooms, and thyme and sauté until tender. Transfer mushroom leek mixture into the bread machine pan. Add remaining ingredients into the bread machine pan. Select basic setting then select medium crust and start. Once loaf is done, remove the loaf pan from the machine. Allow it to cool for 10 minutes. Slice and serve.

Tomato Herb Bread

Servings: 1 Loaf
Cooking Time: 10 Minutes
Ingredients:
- 8 slice bread (1 pounds)
- ½ cup tomato sauce, at 80°F to 90°F
- ½ tablespoon olive oil
- ½ tablespoon sugar
- 1 tablespoon dried basil
- ½ tablespoon dried oregano
- ½ teaspoon salt
- 2 tablespoons grated Parmesan cheese
- 1½ cups white bread flour
- 1⅛ teaspoons bread machine or instant yeast

Directions:
1. Preparing the Ingredients.
2. Choose the size of loaf of your preference and then measure the ingredients.
3. Add all of the ingredients mentioned previously in the list.
4. Close the lid after placing the pan in the bread machine.
5. Select the Bake cycle
6. Turn on the bread machine. Select the White/Basic setting, select the loaf size, and the crust color. Press start.
7. When the cycle is finished, carefully remove the pan from the bread maker and let it rest.
8. Remove the bread from the pan, put in a wire rack to Cool about 5 minutes. Slice

Olive Bread With Italian Herbs

Servings: 8 Pcs
Cooking Time: 1 Hour And 50 Minutes
Ingredients:
- 1 cup (250 ml) water
- ½ cup brine from olives
- Four tablespoons butter
- Three tablespoons sugar
- Two teaspoons salt
- 4 cups flour
- Two teaspoons dry yeast
- ½ cup olives
- One teaspoon Italian herbs

Directions:
1. Add all liquid products. Then add the butter.
2. Fill with brine and water.
3. Add salt and sugar. Gently pour in the flour and pour the dry yeast in the corners on top of the flour.
4. Send the form to the bread maker and wait for the signal before the last dough kneading to add the olives and herbs.

5.   In the meantime, cut olives into 2-3 parts. After the bread maker signals, add it and the Italian herbs into the dough.

6.   Then wait again for the bread maker to signal that the bread is ready.

7.   Cooled Bread has an exciting structure, not to mention the smell and taste. Bon Appetit!

Nutrition Info: Calories: 332 Cal;Fat: 7.5 g;Cholesterol: 15 g;Sodium: 749 mg;Carbohydrates: 55.5 g;Fiber: 3

Chocolate-cherry Bread

Servings: 1 Loaf
Cooking Time: 10 Minutes
Ingredients:
- 1½ teaspoons baking powder
- ½ teaspoon baking soda
- ¼ teaspoon salt
- ¾ cup sugar
- ½ cup butter, softened
- 2 eggs
- 1 teaspoon almond extract
- 1 teaspoon vanilla
- 1 container (8 oz) sour cream
- ½ cup chopped dried cherries
- ½ cup bittersweet or dark chocolate chips

Directions:
1.   Preparing the Ingredients.
2.   Choose the size of loaf of your preference and then measure the ingredients.
3.   Add all of the ingredients mentioned previously in the list. Close the lid after placing the pan in the bread machine.
4.   Select the Bake cycle
5.   Turn on the bread machine. Select the White/Basic setting, select the loaf size, and the crust color. Press start.
6.   When the cycle is finished, carefully remove the pan from the bread maker and let it rest.
7.   Remove the bread from the pan, put in a wire rack to cool for at least 2 hours. Wrap tightly and store at room temperature up to 4 days, or refrigerate.

Basil Tomato Bread

Servings: 14 Slices
Cooking Time: 10 Minutes
Ingredients:
- 2¼ tsp dried active baking yeast
- 1⅝ cups bread flour
- 3 Tbsp wheat bran
- 5 Tbsp quinoa
- 3 Tbsp dried milk powder
- 1 Tbsp dried basil
- 25g sun-dried tomatoes, chopped

- 1 tsp salt
- 1⅛ cups water
- 1 cup boiling water to cover tomatoes

Directions:
1. Preparing the Ingredients.
2. Cover dried tomatoes with boiling water in a bowl.
3. Soak for 10 minutes, drain, and cool to room temperature.
4. Snip tomatoes into small pieces, using scissors.
5. Add each ingredient to the bread machine in the order and at the temperature recommended by your bread machine manufacturer.
6. Select the Bake cycle
7. Close the lid, select the basic bread, medium crust setting on your bread machine and press start.
8. When the bread machine has finished baking, remove the bread and put it on a cooling rack.

Cranberry Honey Bread

Servings: 1 Loaf

Ingredients:
- 16 slice bread (2 pounds)
- 1¼ cups + 1 tablespoon lukewarm water
- ¼ cup unsalted butter, melted
- 3 tablespoons honey or molasses
- 4 cups white bread flour
- ½ cup cornmeal
- 2 teaspoons table salt
- 2½ teaspoons bread machine yeast
- ¾ cup cranberries, dried
- 12 slice bread (1½ pounds)
- 1 cup + 1 tablespoon lukewarm water
- 2 tablespoons unsalted butter, melted
- 3 tablespoons honey or molasses
- 3 cups white bread flour
- ⅓ cup cornmeal
- 1½ teaspoons table salt
- 2 teaspoons bread machine yeast
- ½ cup cranberries, dried

Directions:
1. Choose the size of loaf you would like to make and measure your ingredients.
2. Add all of the ingredients except for the dried cranberries to the bread pan in the order listed above.
3. Place the pan in the bread machine and close the lid.
4. Turn on the bread maker. Select the White/Basic or Fruit/Nut (if your machine has this setting) setting, then the loaf size, and finally the crust color. Start the cycle.
5. When the machine signals to add ingredients, add the dried cranberries. (Some machines have a fruit/nut hopper where you can add the dried cranberries when you start the machine. The machine will automatically add them to the dough during the baking process.)

6. When the cycle is finished and the bread is baked, carefully remove the pan from the machine. Use a potholder as the handle will be very hot. Let rest for a few minutes.

7. Remove the bread from the pan and allow to cool on a wire rack for at least 10 minutes before slicing.

Nutrition Info: (Per Serving):Calories 174, fat 2.6 g, carbs 33.6 g, sodium 310 mg, protein 4 g

Orange Bread

Servings: 1 Loaf
Cooking Time: 10 Minutes
Ingredients:
- 16 slice bread (2 pounds)
- 1¼ cups lukewarm milk
- ¼ cup orange juice
- ¼ cup sugar
- 1½ tablespoons unsalted butter, melted
- 1¼ teaspoons table salt
- 4 cups white bread flour
- Zest of 1 orange
- 1¾ teaspoons bread machine yeast

Directions:
1. Preparing the Ingredients.
2. Choose the size of loaf of your preference and then measure the ingredients.
3. Add all of the ingredients mentioned previously in the list. Close the lid after placing the pan in the bread machine
4. Select the Bake cycle
5. Turn on the bread machine. Select the White/Basic setting, select the loaf size, and the crust color. Press start.
6. When the cycle is finished, carefully remove the pan from the bread maker and let it rest.
7. Remove the bread from the pan, put in a wire rack to cool. Cool completely, about 10 minutes. Slice

Blueberry Bread

Servings: 10
Cooking Time: 2 Hours
Ingredients:
- Milk – ¾ cup.
- Egg – 1
- Water – 3 tbsps.
- Butter – 2 tbsps.
- Sugar – 3 tbsps.
- Salt – ¾ tsp.
- Ground nutmeg – ¼ tsp.
- Dried blueberries – 1/3 cup.
- Bread flour – 3 cups.
- Active dry yeast – 1 tsp.

Directions:
1. Add all ingredients into the bread machine pan. Select basic setting then select medium crust and start. Once loaf is done, remove the loaf pan from the machine. Allow it to cool for 10 minutes. Slice and serve.

Strawberry Oat Bread

Servings: 1 Loaf
Cooking Time: 10 Minutes
Ingredients:
*   16 slice bread (2 pounds)
*   1½ cups lukewarm milk
*   ¼ cup unsalted butter, melted
*   ¼ cup sugar
*   2 teaspoons table salt
*   1½ cups quick oats
*   3 cups white bread flour
*   2 teaspoons bread machine yeast
*   1 cup strawberries, sliced

Directions:
1. Preparing the Ingredients.
2. Choose the size of loaf of your preference and then measure the ingredients.
3. Add all of the ingredients mentioned previously in the list, except for the strawberries. Close the lid after placing the pan in the bread machine.
4. Select the Bake cycle
5. Turn on the bread machine. White/Basic or Fruit/Nut (if your machine has this setting) setting, select the loaf size, and the crust color. Press start.
6. When the machine signals to add ingredients, add the strawberries. When the cycle is finished, carefully remove the pan from the bread maker and let it rest.
7. Remove the bread from the pan, put in a wire rack to cool for at least 10 minutes, and slice.

CPSIA information can be obtained
at www.ICGtesting.com
Printed in the USA
LVHW101400050421
683476LV00034B/1269